Searching For Matilda

Portrait of a Forgotten Feminist

*"There is a word sweeter than
mother, home, or heaven —
that word is Liberty"*

By Charlotte M. Shapiro

D1563800

ISBN-13 978-0615772325
LCCN 2013903494

Published by CreateSpace

DEDICATION

To my friends and colleagues
who inspired and collaborated with
me to pursue the feminist ideals and
values that enriched my life:
Lore Jarmul, Marilyn Sternberg,
Lillian McCormick and Claire Stern.

It was a feminist journey immeasurably supported
and shared by my loving husband and life companion,
Marvin Shapiro, who encouraged me at every turn,
aware that it was changing our lives.

And to my cherished children and grandchildren:
Rick, Susan, Jill, Dale, Penny, Adam, Leo, Blake and Ben,
who have already chosen or are about to choose
rewarding journeys of their own.

ACKNOWLEDGEMENTS

I am truly grateful for the special care and enthusiasm with which editor and author, **Lynn Povich** enriched the manuscript for this book. Her questions and suggestions enlivened the story of Matilda Joslyn Gage beyond her historical presence. As a journalist, feminist and pioneer activist for women's equal employment rights in the 1970's, Lynn Povich offered her insight into Matilda Joslyn Gage's relevance for women today.

My great appreciation also goes to **Jill Norgren**, historian and professor emeritus of John Jay College. As the author of *Belva Lockwood: The Woman Who Would be President*, Jill Norgren provided her special knowledge of the historic period in which Gage lived. Her expertise helped me refine Gage's role in the 19th century woman's equal rights movement.

A special thank you goes to **Sally Roesch Wagner**, Executive Director of the Matilda Joslyn Gage Foundation, who was most kind and supportive of my efforts to write this bibliographical study.

This book also belongs to **Jill DeGroff**, graphic artist, author, caricaturist and treasured daughter. Jill provided her technical expertise, creative book design and tender loving care to the entire process of this book's production. I am forever grateful.

Thank you to my friends who read Matilda in its early rendition and offered their reactions, suggestions and generous support: Claire Stern, Joan and David Cooper, Arlene Soifer and Rhoda Ashley.

CONTENTS

PART I
OMISSION FROM HISTORY

A Question of History   7

Erased From the Record   11

Anthony's Midnight Coup   15

Conflict Among the Leaders   19

Neglect By Male Historians   24

Anthony Dominates the Record   25

Gage's Criticism of the Church   27

PART II
MATILDA, THE WOMAN

Her Early Years   29

Humanist and Egalitarian   33

Feminist Historian   37

Her Search for the Spiritual   41

Feminist: Both Passionate and Radical   43

Intellectual, Scholar and Theorist   47

PART III

LOOKING BACK

Femininity, Feminism and Sex   49

The Suffragists' Legacy   52

PART IV

REFLECTIONS

On the Writing of History   57

On Pursuing a Parent's Cause   59

On Feminism   60

On Advocacy and its Unintended Consequences   61

BIBLIOGRAPHY   63

INTERNET REFERENCES   92

END PAPERS

Timeline   95

Last Will   97

Obituary   101

PART I
OMISSION FROM HISTORY
A Question of History

"Matilda Joslyn Gage was just as important as Susan B. Anthony and Elizabeth Cady Stanton to the 19th century woman suffrage movement," were the words of a lecturer who spoke with great authority. She addressed a group of retirees attending an Elderhostel in upstate New York, whose faces betrayed their disbelief. No one in that well educated audience had ever heard of Matilda Joslyn Gage.

Downstate New York skeptics were not inclined to believe a speaker from a sleepy town upstate. Moreover, everyone knew that Susan B. Anthony was the undisputed hero of the suffrage movement. The Gage woman that the lecturer described must have been a local feminist activist in the nearby community of Fayetteville where the Gage house still stands. Fayetteville Is close to Syracuse and Seneca Falls, the New York town famous for the first women's equal rights convention in 1848.

If Matilda Joslyn Gage really was an exceptional leader in suffrage history, then how could that name have escaped me during thirteen years of teaching high school American Studies? For more than twenty years, I had been steeped in feminist literature while working for women's equal employment rights. The challenge to find out the facts about Matilda Joslyn Gage was irresistible.

An initial search in an old college textbook, Samuel Eliot Morrison's *Oxford History of the American People* (1965) the "gold standard" of history texts, found no mention of Matilda Joslyn Gage. Worse, Morrison gave the suffrage movement all of two sentences under "Bootleggers and Other Sports" while he devoted three entire pages to Prohibition and its repeal with the 20th Amendment!

Neither did Gage appear in a current high school text. Susan B. Anthony and suffrage were given a brief entry under, "Reformers and Self-Helpers," with an iconic photo of the women, all dressed in white, marching in the 1913 suffrage parade in Washington D.C. A more generous description of Jane Addams and the Settlement House movement followed. Social work, more ladylike than equal rights demands, deserved more attention.

Was Matilda Joslyn Gage really excluded from history? And if so, why? How vital was she to the 19th century woman's suffrage movement?

Did the Elderhostel speaker exaggerate the historic prominence Gage deserved? A bibliographical search in history books and biographies might uncover reliable facts. Little did I expect that searching for Matilda would become a three year long research project!

Many stories emerged about the suffragists' interpersonal relationships and the not-so-friendly conflicts in the history by-passed by traditional male historians. Matilda and other prominent activists had to wait their turn on the pages of history until women biographers and historians uncovered them in the 1980's.

Prior to 1980, histories and biographies of the women's reform movement had almost no recognition of Gage. She was invisible with one surprising exception: a work published in 1893 while she was still alive! Gage's biography appears in A *WOMAN OF THE CENTURY: 1470 Biographical Sketches Accompanied by Portraits of Leading American Women in All Walks of Life.* Mary Livermore, one of the two editors, was a contemporary suffragist and friend.

There were only brief references to Matilda Joslyn Gage scattered in books published between 1980 and 2000, with the exception of William Leach's 1980 book, *True Love and Perfect Union.* Leach   praised Gage's stature. "Her work, he wrote, "was at the frontiers of progressive thought." But Matilda Joslyn Gage's name and thought have not yet broken through the wall that conceals her to popular history.

Recognition of Gage as feminist theorist, historian and suffragist leader is still well hidden in the 21st century despite the significant research and publications of two contemporary academicians: Sally Roesch Wagner and Leila Brammer.

Fortunately, the Connecticut University and State Library Systems offered rich resources for probing the mystery of Matilda Joslyn Gage and the time in which she lived.

*Attached to this publication is an annotated bibliography of the 50 books and internet references used in searching for Matilda. Since this is a bibliographical study, not an academic paper, there are references to authors, but no footnotes. The author's name will be found in parentheses after a quotation or specific opinion and can be referenced in the bibliography.

Erased From the Record

The original record of the 19th century woman's equal rights movement that historians use are the first three volumes of the History of Woman Suffrage edited by Susan B. Anthony, Elizabeth Cady Stanton and Matilda Joslyn Gage. Despite her name as an editor, Gage is a minor presence there. Anthony and Stanton, Gage's close associates, marginalized her in the History of Woman Suffrage, making her invisible. Articles Gage had written were omitted. Others failed to identify her as the author. (Brammer)

Omitted was her acclaimed and original speech on women's achievements throughout civilization. Gage's very first public speech, given at the 1852 Syracuse Convention, received such a great reception that it was the only one printed for distribution. Her speech identified the many exceptional women throughout the history of civilization which she said proved that women were equal to men.

Stanton and Anthony placed substantial biographies of themselves in the History but wrote only a brief biography of Matilda in a footnote. The History's index devoted a full page of citations for Anthony, two-thirds page for Stanton and one-fourth page for Gage. Matilda Joslyn Gage, the movement's intellectual theorist and scholar, was well concealed from suffrage history. (Brammer)

The suffrage "triumvirate," Anthony, Stanton and Gage," decided to write the historical record of their reform movement as an afterthought. Almost thirty years had passed since the first equal rights convention in 1848 In Seneca Falls. The women set to work in 1876 at Stanton's home in Tenafly, New Jersey, where

Stanton was then living. It was an enormous task to collect and read the records, correspondence and documents stored in so many places. (Wagner)

The three women had signed an agreement. Stanton and Gage would "write, collect, select and arrange material." Anthony, who disliked writing intensely, would be the "business agent" to finance and secure publication. All three names would appear on the title page, share the copyright and share the profits. (Griffith, Wagner, Lutz)

Pushing Gage to the margins of the written record occurred over several years. Anthony first announced that she and Stanton were preparing a history of their reform movement at a National Woman's Suffrage Association (NWSA) Convention. Gage, who chaired the meeting, was surprised that her name was omitted, but said nothing. When her name was not mentioned on another occasion, Stanton chided Gage for not confronting Anthony. And when Stanton and Anthony were interviewed by a reporter from the *New York Herald*, they "forgot" to name their associate Matilda Joslyn Gage. The omission of Gage was completed when Susan B. Anthony and editor, Ida Husted Harper excluded Gage from Volume IV of the History of Woman Suffrage.

Anthony had commissioned journalist Harper to write Volume IV of the *History* as a supplement to the other three volumes. It was designed to include the events and information which Anthony, alone, chose to preserve. After the two women completed their work, Anthony deliberately burned all the correspondence and documents in her possession - papers that would have been invaluable to historians.

References to the *History of Woman Suffrage* almost always refer only to Volumes I to III. Volume IV is criticized as "full of pageantry, pomp, and even floral decorations." The last two volumes, V and VI, edited by Harper and written after the founders' deaths, are dismissed as public relations. (Weatherford)

Were Gage's associates insensitive to the way they treated her?

Were their actions deliberate? Matilda's work in Tenafly had been cut short in order to return to Fayetteville to care for her sick husband. Nevertheless, Gage had continued her work at home, coming to Tenafly whenever possible for a month at a time. In turn, Anthony made a sufficient number of business trips to Gage's home to have her name now placed on the room where she had stayed. Visitors to the Fayetteville house, a museum, can explore that room among the exhibits.

Anthony and Stanton may not have been malicious, but their actions distorted the historic record. Historians of suffrage reform used three primary works in their research: the *History of Woman Suffrage*, Harper's authorized biography of Anthony and Stanton's autobiography, *Eighty Years and More*. As a result, historians perpetuated Matilda's absence from the literature.

Hidden were Gage's original theories on patriarchy, men's power over church and state to subjugate women. Hidden, too, were her feminist analyses of history and society. "Ideas that took her a lifetime to construct had to be recreated through a similar painstaking process by second wave feminist theorists." (Brammer)

Gage's condemnation of patriarchy still resonates today as women's reproductive health is threatened with loss of public financial support. Opposition to freedom of choice comes from patriarchy, men's power in the church and halls of government.

Leila Brammer wrote that Gage's "exclusion was not personal but the result of a complex political process that pushed the issues she thought important to the sidelines." Yet the many sources reviewed in this bibliographical study point to Gage's exclusion as both political and personal.

Handbill from competing suffrage association.
Speakers included Lucy Stone and huband
Henry Blackwell.

Anthony's Midnight Coup

With astute political skill, Anthony successfully merged two opposing and competing suffrage organizations while Gage was absent, unable to defend the integrity and principles upon which their organization had been founded. The first suffrage organization was the National Woman Suffrage Association (NWSA) founded by Anthony, Stanton and Gage in New York in 1869. The second was the American Woman Suffrage Association (AWSA) founded by Lucy Stone in Boston six months later. Why two national suffrage organizations? It was the result of the intense conflict over the 15th Amendment to the Constitution which guaranteed the vote only for former male slaves. Still excluded were women, both white and black. National opposed the 15th Amendment, American supported it.

NWSA women were outraged that the 15th Amendment failed to include the vote for women. As white women, their hot anger frequently turned racist. Congress was denounced for its denial of justice. AWSA women, on the other hand, supported the 15th Amendment. They believed the Negro vote had to take precedence in deference to the Civil War that had been fought to free the slaves. Suffragists would have to be "patient;" their turn would come.

Suffrage activists also split over the political strategies needed to secure the vote. The National Association insisted suffrage required Congress to pass a federal law, a Constitutional Amendment, while the American Association believed that suffrage would require separate passage by each of the states.

Twenty years had gone by since those two associations had been founded. Anthony was determined that the two merge into one in order to enlarge the movement. She knew that both Matilda Joslyn Gage and Elizabeth Cady Stanton were strongly opposed to the merger because of their serious ideological differences. The American Association's membership now included women from the Women's Christian Temperance Union (WCTU) an organization that was lobbying not only for temperance but also for prayer in the public schools and blue laws to observe the Sabbath. Both religious and conservative, WCTU had decided to support suffrage only to advance its own Christian mission.

Gage and Stanton feared the growing power of evangelical women who would destroy the First Amendment's guarantee of separation of church and state. It was inevitable that WCTU's conservative members would subvert and revise National's program and principles.

Anthony literally carried out a midnight coup. The Convention that night had dragged on with its parliamentary business, losing more and more attendees until the evening threatened to become morning. Only 30 members were left to vote for the merger.

Anthony engineered the merger in Gage's absence by removing opponents from the Executive Committee that Gage chaired. Gage, who was visiting her son in the Dakota Territory, was unable to attend the Convention. She accused Anthony of taking advantage of her unavoidable absence…with good reason. Anthony had denied Gage the transportation money she needed to get to Washington, money that was ordinarily available to officers of the organization.

Gage charged Susan B. Anthony with "manipulating and undermining NWSA members." (Barry) It was nothing short of betrayal. Gage called it "treachery."

But Anthony's overriding mission was to enlarge the suffrage tent. It did not matter what a member's politics or religion was. All those who supported woman suffrage were welcome. The single issue of the vote had been a unifying strategy for many years. It would continue to be the exclusive goal of the combined associations with the added clout of their increased membership. WCTU had 150,000 members; NWSA 13,000. (Ward and Burns) Consistent with Anthony's leadership in the past, pragmatism would always trump principle.

Gage retaliated. She established a new organization: the Woman's National Liberal Union (WNLU) and presided as president. Anthony was furious. Gage's action was more than a radical response; it was a defiance that enraged Anthony. She wrote letters to their suffragist friends and members of National heatedly urging them to boycott Gage's new organization.

Fear of competition from WNLU was unnecessary. The new organization attracted those on the fringe of progressivism: anarchists, freethinkers, reformers of every stripe, who joined together in their dedication to separation of church and state. WNLU had the benefit of substantial financial support at the beginning but then languished for eight years for lack of funds.

Elizabeth Cady Stanton had also opposed the merger. She was as vigilant and concerned as Matilda Joslyn Gage about safeguarding separation of church and state. She had given Gage tacit support for initiating a new organization. No matter. Stanton had grown tired and indifferent to organization politics. Always independent, she would not let Anthony's strategy imperil their friendship.

Anthony persuaded the merged National American Woman Suffrage Association (NAWSA) to accept Stanton's presidency instead of her own. Stanton, whose presidency was honorary, soon sailed for England, where her daughter and family were living. Her absence would not be a problem. Elizabeth had lost no time raising the issue of divorce and the church's suppression of women – issues that were anathema to the conservative members now dominant in NAWSA. Stanton's presidency did not protect her from NAWSA's condemnation as a heretic when she published her book, *The Woman's Bible*.

Elizabeth Cady Stanton

Susan B. Anthony

Conflict Among the Leaders

The treatment of Gage by her closest colleagues raises many questions about her relationship with Susan B. Anthony and Elizabeth Cady Stanton.

It was clear that Matilda Joslyn Gage was peripheral to Stanton and Anthony's exceedingly close friendship. Biographies of Stanton and Anthony reveal an uncommon devotion to each other, an unusual closeness. The two women had met and become good friends in 1851 at a Temperance meeting.

Anthony and Stanton had worked together in Amelia Bloomer's New York Temperance Society. Temperance organizations, a forerunner to suffrage, attracted large numbers of women. Alcohol was the curse of many a marriage. It was responsible for domestic violence, immorality and precious money squandered. Wives had no legal redress; divorce was not an option. (There was no explanation for why Amelia Bloomer's name became attached to a dress consisting of pantaloons covered by a loose smock. The Bloomer was a radical challenge to the stiff corseted dress that restricted and injured women's bodies. It met with contempt and rejection for those who were brave enough to wear it. Women soon abandoned that comfortable dress and succumbed to the accepted costume of the day.)

Anthony and Stanton's unusual bonding would not have been possible to predict. Susan B. Anthony was an unmarried woman of modest Quaker, middle class background while Elizabeth Cady Stanton was married, from a wealthy Presbyterian family, the mother of seven children, and five years Anthony's senior. Susan was something of a "Plain Jane" while Elizabeth was an attractive, fashionable woman with a head of curls, the envy of any woman.

Anthony was "Aunt Susan" to the Stanton children. She stayed at Elizabeth's home with great frequency for long periods of time to work on suffrage affairs, and help with the seven young, rambunctious children in Henry Stanton's absence. Husband Henry's work as abolitionist, attorney, and political activist kept him away from home a great deal of the time. He was aware of his wife's partnership with Anthony and that she wrote Susan's speeches. Much amused, Henry told Elizabeth, "You stir up Susan and she stirs the world." (DuBois Correspondence)

When they were apart, Anthony and Stanton constantly wrote letters to each other. Their correspondence over fifty years of friendship and collaboration filled five volumes of a thousand pages each with a sixth volume just off the press! (Gordon)

The two women traveled together on Lyceum lecture tours whenever their speech assignments permitted. Stanton had spent eleven years, eight months a year on the lecture "circuit" to pay for her children's college tuitions. They also vacationed together. When Stanton had been in England with her family, Anthony joined her for a long rest and tour of the European Continent.

Elizabeth Cady Stanton dedicated her autobiography, *Eighty Years and More, Reminiscences 1815-1897*, to Susan B. Anthony, "my steadfast friend for half a century." Neither spouse nor children are in the dedication. Husband Henry is barely mentioned.

The Stanton children placed Aunt Susan's photograph on top of their mother's casket.

Matilda Joslyn Gage was outside that friendship. In education, intellect, and ideology, Yet Gage and Stanton had much more in common with each other than with Anthony. They were both dedicated to the cause of expanding human rights, critical of the church's subordination of women, and interested in spiritual alternatives to organized religion. More than Anthony, Gage and Stanton shared an intense feminist ideology, benefited from a superior education, and had fathers who had educated them on legal and social issues. (Gage's father a physician and scholar; Stanton's father a lawyer and judge.)

Friendships have an intangible chemistry, immune to objective analysis. Although Gage was peripheral to the Stanton/Anthony friendship, the three women shared mutual respect and commitment to suffrage activism. Anthony and Stanton respected Gage's scholarship. In her autobiography, Stanton wrote that Gage "had a knack of rummaging through old libraries, bringing more startling facts to light than any woman I ever knew." (The word "rummaging," reveals a rather uncomplimentary edge.)

Anthony frequently consulted Gage when a policy or factual difference with Stanton had to be reconciled. She would plead with Gage to "scan the law and the logic" of her friend's position, one that she opposed. "If she and you see the matter alike - I shall surrender," Anthony wrote in a letter to Gage. (Ginzberg)

The three women were not really a team; they functioned as individuals. It was inevitable that one of them would emerge as leader-in-chief. It was Anthony, the prime organizer, not the two writer-intellectuals.

Gage could be assertive and outspoken, but still maintain a modest sense of self in contrast to Stanton who was described as "egotistical, elitist, intolerant" proud of her brilliance as a writer and public speaker. "She was absolutist, cutting about women she considered less brilliant, less radical or less self-confident than she." (Ginzberg) When the 15th Amendment gave the vote to former male slaves, but not to women, Stanton referred to the "ignorant Sambo" and declared that the right to vote should be reserved to those who were educated.

Stanton's feelings toward Gage were evident in her autobiography *Eighty Years and More*. Considering that Stanton and Gage had worked together for 40 years, the content that included Gage is surprisingly brief. She appears in the book at the 1876 Centennial Celebration in Philadelphia where Stanton writes that they "worked sixteen hour days." She recalled how Gage held an umbrella over Anthony's head to protect her from

July's blazing sun while she read the "Woman's Declaration of Independence." (It is a story repeated in so many of the books.) Stanton also credited Gage's assistance to Anthony before her trial for voting illegally. So much for the positive content of Matilda's presence in Eighty Years and More.

The negative content was subtle. Elizabeth did not hide her disdain for Matilda's complaint that she had signed autographs using Matilda's original and favorite motto without attribution. She gives Matilda a back-handed apology. Use of her motto, Elizabeth wrote, was just a "misunderstanding." The motto: "There is a word sweeter than Mother, Home or Heaven – that word is Liberty," originated as Gage's retort to WCTU president Frances Willard who proclaimed that the virtues of Mother, Home and Heaven surpassed all others. The motto was placed on Matilda's tombstone by her children.

Finally, Elizabeth Cady Stanton's autobiography glossed over her failure to credit Gage for the contribution she made to her book, *The Woman's Bible*. Stanton had invited Gage to collaborate on the book, then reneged on her promise to include Gage in the book's copyright. Omitted from Stanton's autobiography was her response to Gage's distraught letter asking that Stanton re-submit the copyright of *The Woman's Bible* to include both their names. Stanton's response was to offer Gage $100 as compensation. (Kern) The contrast between Stanton's brief comments about Gage in her book and the lengthy, affectionate description of her friendship with Anthony is palpable.

Susan B. Anthony's official biography was somewhat more generous in her references to Matilda. She recognized Gage's valuable work but did not award her the prominence she deserved. The two women had had many years of close collaboration in NWSA before their rupture over the merger of the two suffrage associations.

Anthony's diary has interesting bits of gossip about Gage, reproduced in Barry's 1988 biography of Susan B. Anthony.

Matilda is "irritable" … "feels overshadowed"… is a dear good woman…but desperately misanthropic – distrusts everybody's loyalty to her." Matilda didn't return Susan's kiss on one occasion, "but turned her cheek." Petty irritations may have been blown out of proportion due to the limitations of correspondence. Remember, these women had no telephone, no e-mail, no Facebook, no Twitter, only letters and meetings.

Yet Matilda may not have been that easy to get along with. Gage historian Sally Roesch Wagner writes that Matilda "had gained a reputation for four qualities. She was principled to a fault. She was brilliant. She was fearless in stating her beliefs. And she did not suffer fools gladly." Helen Gage described her mother as impulsive, energetic, fearless, self-reliant." The record suggests that Matilda was unyielding in her pursuit of justice. "Conciliation was not a word in Gage's vocabulary." (Wagner)

At the end, Matilda's departure from her suffragist colleagues was explosive. The divisive politics around the merger of the two suffrage organizations had a long reach into the many years of their work together. Gage's bitter words in a letter to her friend Lillie Devereux Blake revealed the depth of her estrangement: "It has always been the policy of Susan & Stanton to play into each other's hands and to hold each other up at the expense of all other workers." (Gordon)

Had she written an autobiography, Matilda Joslyn Gage might not have been invisible to history. But this dedicated historian of women's accomplishments over the ages neglected to write her own history. Research, writing and political activism dominated her life, taking precedence over what she may have considered self-promotion.

Gage was careful, however, to preserve her valued writings. Her will specified that her "scrapbooks" be placed in a permanent library; her papers be left in care of daughter Maud. The Gage scrapbooks are in the Library of Congress; other papers are located in several university and regional libraries.

Neglect by Male Historians

Matilda Joslyn Gage's omission from history can also be laid at the door of male historians who failed to take the full measure of the 19th century suffrage movement. Historian Samuel Eliot Morrison, for example, dismissed suffrage as a far less significant reform movement compared to prohibition because, he said, prohibition had far-reaching social and political influence. Perhaps more significant was that women and suffrage did not fit well into history writing tradition, a tradition that focused on political, economic and military events, all male domains. So the history of suffrage became "a watered down account." (Brammer)

The original explanation for Gage's omission from history, of course, was her invisibility in the *History of Woman Suffrage*. But when feminist historians extended the frontiers of history to include social history Matilda Joslyn Gage's name started appearing. Women's correspondence, diaries, and memoirs, as well as local newspapers' archives became treasured sources of information for feminist historians. At first, scholarly works on women's history in the 1970's were devoted to women's private lives. (DuBois) Histories of the political dimensions of the women's reform efforts and influence on public policy came later.

The first publication to restore Matilda Joslyn Gage to mainstream history was Sally Roesch Wagner's monograph, *She Who Holds the Sky*, published in 1998. Soon afterwards, Gage's book *Woman, Church and State*, originally published in 1893, was re-issued in 2002 with a special Introduction by Wagner. At last Matilda's original theories and analysis of history were current but too late to have helped the work of "second wave" feminists in the 1970's.

Also available to present-day readers is the utopian vision of society that Matilda inspired in her son-in-law's *Wizard of Oz* books, but how many people would recognize that?

Anthony Dominates the Record

If Matilda Joslyn Gage's angry exit from the merged suffrage associations, omissions from the History of Woman Suffrage, the leadership conflicts, and the neglect of historians were not sufficient to exclude her from history, the deed was accomplished by the dominance of Susan B. Anthony. She overshadowed both Gage and Stanton. "Anthony's power in NWSA pushed Gage into the recesses of the public face of the movement." (Wagner)

Susan B. Anthony had national visibility from many decades of speechmaking across the country and the enormous publicity of her arrest and trial for voting illegally. She had been front and center of the suffrage movement for more than fifty years, the elder stateswoman, the popular "Aunt Susan" for the young generation that followed.

Anthony had the distinct advantage of not having married (the "old maid" pejorative notwithstanding). Unlike Gage and Stanton, she had freedom from the responsibilities of husband and children. Nor did she have to be a legal appendage to a husband. Anthony found little sympathy for family interference with her agenda. She chided "Mrs. Stanton" (never Elizabeth) for becoming pregnant with child number seven.

After the merger of NWSA and AWSA, Gage and Stanton were no longer active in the movement. The reform movement had changed. Susan B. Anthony was politically safe, untainted by the radical positions taken by Gage and Stanton. She was a middle-of-the-roader, supported by conservative women, moderate women and religious women. "Anthony steered clear of controversy." (Kern)

The suffrage amendment to the Constitution, originally written by Stanton, was re-named the Anthony Amendment. Not a word had been changed. But neither Stanton nor Anthony had been able to achieve its passage. The Amendment languished in Congress for more than 30 years before it won passage in 1920 as the 19th Amendment to the Constitution. Women had to wait 72 years from that first meeting at Seneca Falls for the right to vote!

As a result of her book, *The Woman's Bible,* Elizabeth Cady Stanton's name went into the dark corners of history for more than 60 years. The condemnation of *The Woman's Bible* had to have been a terrible blow because Stanton had had immense popularity and admiration as a public speaker and writer. Members of NAWSA, denounced Stanton's book as sacrilegious despite Anthony's efforts to protect her dear friend. The women were deaf to Stanton's explanation that the book was a revised reading of women in the Bible; an attempt to restore woman's status in Christianity. Stanton became the "first victim of NAWSA's emphasis on unity, hostility to dissent, and implicit conservatism." (DuBois Correspondence)

Stanton's daughter, Harriot Stanton Blatch, tried to restore her mother to her rightful place in history. Success eluded her. She and her brother Theodore published their mother's letters, diary and reminiscences to no avail. Not until 36 years after her death was the first biography of Stanton written, in 1940, by Alma Lutz, who benefited greatly from Harriot's assistance. But it took three more decades until Stanton's immense contribution to the struggle for women's equality was acclaimed by "second wave" feminists in the 1970's.

Alone in the spotlight, Anthony was left to dominate the suffrage landscape, anointed by the men who wrote history. She became the icon for suffrage that will always prevail. "Beloved Aunt Susan," was commemorated with the Anthony dollar by President Jimmy Carter. Issued in 1978, it is no longer in circulation.

Gage's Criticism of the Church

Matilda Joslyn Gage was intensely angry at the injustice she believed the church had inflicted upon woman. Patriarchy, with its domination of the church and Christianity, deliberately made woman inferior and man superior because woman was responsible for original sin in the Garden of Eden. That was how the church justified the necessity for woman's subservience to man. Woman was denied the priesthood as well as any meaningful role in fulfilling the church's spiritual mission.

Although the very radical anti-church resolutions, introduced by Gage and Stanton at suffrage conventions from 1878 to 1885 were defeated, other anti-church resolutions increased the antagonism many clergy already had for suffrage and for women who betrayed "true womanhood." Anthony feared that Gage's criticism of the church would subvert suffrage success. (Brammer)

Conflict with the clergy had arisen earlier after the 1852 Syracuse Convention. The local press printed letters-to-the-editor between local ministers and "Anonymous" which disputed or contradicted the meaning of Biblical quotations. Quarrels about the Bible and the proper role of woman in society, argued back and forth in the letters, became a source of amusement for the newspaper's readers. "Anonymous" turned out to be Matilda Joslyn Gage. (Wagner)

The women's challenges to biblical interpretation appeared to be less sinful than their behavior. The ministers upbraided the women for conduct they said was immoral, sacrilegious and unnatural. Suffragists had defiled the sanctity of home and hearth. "True womanhood" required a woman to be "domestic, maternal, religious, cultured and subservient."(Griffith) For women to join together at public meetings and demand equal rights with men was the work of Satan.

The clergy's condemnation was not new. The same charges about woman's "rightful sphere" and the sanctity of home and family had been leveled against the women years before when they spoke out in public at abolition meetings.

Gage's criticism of the church became increasingly radical. Her radicalism had peaked with the publication of *Woman, Church and State* in 1893, three years after she had angrily closed the door on her twenty years of leadership in the National Woman's Suffrage Association. Published at a time when conservatism flourished, *Woman, Church and State* ran afoul of the law on obscenity.

The obscenity law, passed in 1873, chose a very broad view to identify obscenity. It was a crime to mail any material considered obscene, lewd or lascivious, material that included information on birth control, abortion, physiology, and sex education. Anthony Comstock, for whom the law was named, was an illustrious crusader against vice, drunkenness, pornography and sex in any and all of its manifestations. The Carrie Nation of pornography, Comstock rode herd on booksellers and stalked free love practitioners in order to jail all those whose behavior he said defied moral standards; moral standards for which he was the judge. Victoria Woodhull, suffragist, candidate for president, and free love advocate, was victimized by Comstock and jailed. (Goldsmith, Piercy)

Gage's book had come to Comstock's attention He threatened school board members with arrest if they did not ban *Woman, Church and State* from school libraries. Gage counterattacked in the local press: "Comstock misrepresents all works upon which he presumes to pass judgment, and is as dangerous to liberty of speech and of the press as were the old inquisitors, whom he somewhat resembles." (Wagner) By that time Gage's presence in the suffrage movement had faded.

Actions that had contributed to Gage's exclusion from history had occurred many years earlier. Leila Brammer believes that Gage's "exclusion was not personal but the result of a complex political process that pushed the issues she thought important to the sidelines." Yet the many sources reviewed in this bibliographical study point to Gage's exclusion as both political and personal.

PART II
MATILDA, THE WOMAN
Her Early Years

Reasons for Matilda's exclusion from suffrage history were only part of the mystery. It became compelling to learn about Matilda as a woman; Matilda as a person. More facts about her life could better determine her historic importance. More books and more research!

Matilda Joslyn Gage was the only child of a middle class Baptist family. "From her earliest years, Matilda was accustomed to hearing abstruse political and religious questions discussed." (Willard & Livermore) Her father, Hezekial Joslyn, an esteemed physician and abolitionist, made their home in Manlius, near Syracuse, New York, a safe haven for runaway slaves. The Joslyn house was an intellectual meeting center in the community.

Matilda was home schooled by her father who taught her Greek, Latin, physiology and math. At age 15, she attended Clinton Liberal Institute. Hezekial Joslyn fostered Matilda's independence of thought and to have the courage to support her convictions. Her parents' commitment to high moral standards became hers. When she differed with the family's Baptist minister on one occasion, Matilda did so with her father's full support. It was the freedom to think for herself, to be independent-minded that Matilda valued most in her early education.

The biographical dictionaries generously appraise Gage's father but recognize her mother only for her prestigious Scottish family. But Matilda dedicated her most proud accomplishment, her book, *Woman, Church and State* to her mother "who was at once mother, sister, friend."

Gage devoted her entire life to learning; taught herself Hebrew and advanced Greek in order to read the Bible in the original. Disappointment must have been enormous for both Matilda and her father when his connections and influence in the medical establishment could not overcome gender barriers to her admission to medical school.

Matilda was eighteen when she married Henry Gage, a dry goods merchant eight years her senior. Although eighteen would not have been considered young for marriage in the 1840's, Matilda's ambition and superior education might have led her to postpone marriage for a few years. Motherhood followed within ten months. Birth control literature and contraceptives at the time were scarce and difficult to obtain.

Matilda had four children: three daughters and one son. Another son had died soon after birth. She was very devoted to her children and solicitous of her husband's health. When Henry Gage took ill, Matilda suspended her work at Stanton's home in New Jersey to return to Fayetteville, leaving Stanton to continue writing the *History of Woman Suffrage*.

During Henry's two year long illness, Matilda assumed full responsibility for managing Henry's store, worked on the History when time permitted and provided home weddings for two daughters within 19 months. Matilda herself coped with bouts of illness. Therefore, Elizabeth Cady Stanton is credited with writing most of Volume II.

Henry's role in the family is a mystery. One story describes young Henry Gage having built "an isolation house" for the sick during a cholera epidemic in Syracuse. (Dictionary of American Biography) His obituary referred to his interest in politics, though "he gave his first attention to business." (Rivette) In 1870, his estate was valued at $60,000, a considerable sum at that time. But the Gages had serious financial problems later when the economy, Henry's business and health all declined at the same time. Matilda was thought to be the "dominant" partner in the marriage. (American National Biography)

Was Henry Gage supportive of his wife's work? Was he her intellectual equal? No answers. He voted for Democrat Horace Greeley, who failed to support woman suffrage in the 1872 presidential election, while Matilda supported Republican Ulysses S. Grant. The Republican Party appeared to be in support of woman suffrage. It was lip service. Grant's election failed to benefit the suffragists. Forty-eight more years would go by before women won the vote!

Gage lobbied long and hard for women to vote in New York school board elections. We can imagine her exasperation when a State Senator told her that women would be allowed to vote when they were "fit" for it. (O'Neill) Having later won the "fitness" test and the vote in 1880, Gage rounded up all the women in the community to be sure they went to the polls. The result was a clean sweep for women officers for the school board. (Wagner)

Feminist historians who discovered Gage's work are impressed by both her scholarship and feminist theories. Gage was an historian, a prolific writer and political activist. She served as president of both the New York State Suffrage Association and NWSA in 1875. Gage chaired National's Executive Committee for many years and was the editor of its journal "National Citizen and Ballot Box" for three years.

Humanist and Egalitarian

*"The movement for the enfranchisement of women
is the movement for universal humanity."*
— *Gage* (Leach)

Matilda Joslyn Gage was a humanist in the best sense of
that word. She grew up in a family that was humanistic both
in principle and practice. Like her parents, Matilda sheltered
runaway slaves at a time when such action could have put her
in jail and fined her $1000. She advocated for the needs of poor
women when suffragists were focused on the middle class.

Gage joined an auxiliary group of Fayetteville women to prepare
hospital supplies for soldiers during the Civil War. The women
worked many long hours, prompting Matilda to write an article
about that experience. She had been sensitive to the civic
expectations placed on women during the War and believed that
because they were women they received insufficient recognition
and appreciation.

A favorite story about Gage, repeated countless times in many
of the books, was her humanistic impulse to shield Anthony
from the blazing sun while she read the women's Declaration at
the Centennial Celebration in Philadelphia, July 4, 1876. The
famous umbrella story! Stanton, too, related that incident in her
autobiography, aware perhaps that she herself would have been
unlikely to perform the same service.

Gage and Stanton found a living, breathing example of
humanism and equality of the sexes right there in their own
community! The Haudenosaunee (Iroquois) people, members
of the Mohawk Tribe in the Iroquois Confederation, were
neighbors and friends. Native American women had equal
rights with the men in their tribe. The Haudenosaunee had a
matriarchal, egalitarian society - an inspiration for the women's
reform efforts. (Wagner)

Women nominated their tribal chief (though always a man) and had the power to initiate the Chief's removal from office. Custody of children belonged to the mother. Property was communal. Divorce from an irresponsible mate, usually with the family's support, consisted of the man taking his belongings and leaving the longhouse.

This living, contemporary example of a gender equal society was a stark contrast with the one in which Euro-American women lived. Unlike Native American women, they could not easily be freed from an abusive husband, no less choose a president. Rape in Haudenosaunee culture was virtually unknown while rape in American culture brought few men to trial with even fewer convictions.

Gage offered her assistance to the Haudenosaunee when they lobbied against United States efforts to impose American citizenship on their tribes. Citizenship would have denied Native Americans their independence and their recognition as a sovereign nation. Land rights were at stake.

Gratitude earned Gage her adoption into the Wolf Clan of the Mohawks. She received the name Ka-ron-ien-ha-wi, meaning "She Who Holds the Sky." (Wagner)

Gage was the only friend to assist Anthony before her trial for voting illegally in the 1872 election. (Sixteen other women had voted but were not arrested.) Gage and Anthony spoke in every district of New York's Ontario County where the trial was to be held - a speechmaking campaign that had to have been exhausting. Gage gave speeches In 16 districts, entitled, "The U.S. is on Trial, Not Susan B. Anthony." Anthony spoke in 21 districts. (Flexner)

At the trial, the judge chose to write the decision himself, without the judgment of the jury. He brought in a verdict of guilty. The women vilified him. Gage called him a "small-brained, pale-faced, prim-looking man" (who) "with remarkable forethought…penned his decision before hearing the charge." Stanton described the judge as "punctilious in manner, scrupulous in attire, conscientious in trivialities and obtuse on great principles." Contemptuous of the whole proceeding, Anthony refused to pay the fine.

Matilda Joslyn Gage was a good friend and supporter of Belva Lockwood's campaign for president in 1884. Lockwood was a pioneering attorney who had successfully fought for admission to law school and the right to appear in the Supreme Court. She ran for president on the Equal Rights Party Platform as a champion of equal rights for women, Negroes and Native Americans.

The first woman to run for the presidency, Lockwood received 4,149 votes in six states. Gage was an elector-at-large. (Norgren) Neither Anthony nor Stanton participated in Belva Lockwood's campaign for the presidency. For Gage, it was an egalitarian opportunity. She did not support Lockwood's 1888 campaign because she no longer believed it would be educational. In 1888, there were only three states that gave women the right to vote: Utah, Wyoming and Washington. Women could vote in school elections in 14 states. (Norgren)

Although the famous and infamous Victoria Woodhull is usually said to be the first woman to run for president, she was never a viable candidate, nor was her name on the 1872 ballot. She was too young. It is little known Belva Lockwood who, in 1884, was the first woman to run for president.

SPEECH

OF

MRS. M. E. J. GAGE,

AT THE WOMAN'S RIGHTS CONVENTION,

Held at Syracuse, Sept. 1852.

* * * * * This Convention has assembled to discuss the subject of Woman's Rights, and form some settled plan of action for the future. Let Syracuse sustain her name for radicalism. While so much is said of the inferior intellect of woman, it is by a strange absurdity conceded that very many eminent men owe their station in life to their mothers. Women are now in the situation of the mass of mankind, a few years since, when science and learning were in the hands of the priests, and property was held by vassalage; the Pope and the priests claimed to be, not only the teachers, but the guides of the people; the laity were not permitted to examine for themselves; education was held to be unfit for the masses, while the tenure of their landed property was such as kept them in a continual state of dependence on their feudal lord.

* * * It is but a short time, since the most common rudiments of education were deemed sufficient for any woman; could she but read tolerably, and write her own name, it was enough.

* * * Trammeled as women have been, by might and custom, there are still many shining examples, which serve as beacon lights of what may be attained by genius, labor, energy, and perseverance combined. "The longer I live in the world," says Goethe, "the more I am certain, that the great difference between the great, and insignificant, is energy, invincible determination; an honest purpose once fixed, and then victory." Sir Isaac Newton said of himself, "that if ever he had been able to do anything, he had effected it by patient thinking only"; and we are all familiar with the anecdote

Matilda Joslyn Gage's memorable speech at the Syracuse Convention, 1852.

Feminist Historian

"Patriarchy is the foundation for distortions of history.
Freedom for woman underlies all the great questions of the age."
– Gage (Woman, Church and State)

The scene was the Syracuse Convention,1852. Matilda Joslyn Gage attended her first woman's equal rights meeting four years after the famous Seneca Falls Convention where Elizabeth Cady Stanton and Lucretia Mott had issued the historic "Declaration of Rights and Sentiments" in 1848. At age 26, Matilda was the youngest woman there. She had to work up the courage to speak, never having spoken in public before. Was it acceptable to inject herself into the official program? She trembled.

It was Anthony's first equal rights meeting as well. She complained that Matilda's voice was too soft to be heard and asked that the chairperson not permit those who could not raise their voices to speak. (Microphones were not yet invented.) The suggestion was rejected.

Matilda's speech was a huge success. No one ever before had made the case that the history of civilization proved women deserved equal political, economic and social rights. Gage's research uncovered women who had been inventors, scientists, artists, and political leaders. Among women's inventions and accomplishments were bread making, pillow lace, silk, engraving and advances in medicine. In Egypt, infantile diseases were unknown when women dominated the medical profession. The historic content of Gage's speech was unprecedented—a revelation! There was no question that women's creativity, intellect, and achievements proved they were equal to men. Many of the women, whose names and lives Matilda cited, remain extraneous to popular history and literature. Well known are Catherine of Russia, Joan of Arc, but how many people can recognize Christine of Pisa, 14th century author and poet, Queen Margaret of Angouleme, known for her salons, author

Lucrezia Morinella of Venice, artist Artemisia and English feminists Mary Astell and Elizabeth Elstob? (Astell and Elstob were famous during the reign of Queen Anne, the monarch who united England Scotland and Ireland in 1707.)

Lucretia Mott, esteemed Quaker preacher and abolitionist who chaired the Syracuse Convention, was so impressed with Matilda's speech she ordered copies printed for distribution. It is the only one of Gage's speeches for which a text is available.

Not generally remembered, the Seneca Falls Convention had focused on economic and social rights; the right to vote was added at the end. When Elizabeth Cady Stanton introduced the call for a woman's right to vote, it was soundly rejected by many of the people there. Women rushed to remove their names from a petition they had previously signed. Henry Stanton walked out. But the right to vote remained on the record.

Rejecting the vote for women has to be understood within the context of that time. The culture of politics was strictly male. Politics was rowdy, frequently alcohol-driven. Not for a respectable woman! The emphasis on the vote came later, seen as a means for achieving all the other rights. For Susan B. Anthony, the vote became an essential strategy to unify women around a single cause. The many equal rights demanded at Seneca Falls had been too numerous and controversial to get universal support.

Historically, the dominant reform movement in the 1850's was not for a woman's equal rights, it was for the abolition of slavery. Anti-slavery activism had actually been an incubator and training ground for many of the suffragists.

Lucretia Mott and Elizabeth Cady Stanton first met at the World Anti-Slavery Convention in London in 1840. (Stanton went there on her honeymoon.) Mott, Stanton and the other women were barred from the main convention hall. They had to sit in a roped-off observers section. Angered and frustrated, Mott and Stanton commiserated with each other on a park bench where they became fast friends. Although eight years intervened, the discrimination they suffered in London triggered the rebellion at Seneca Falls.

With the outbreak of the Civil War, equal rights advocacy moved to the back burner. Loyalty to the nation came first, so the women organized the Woman's National Loyal League, primarily to press for emancipation but also to organize and supply soldiers with hospital supplies and materials they needed. Always totally committed to a cause she adopted, Gage's wartime work was so outstanding it was later honored by Fayetteville. Not until after the Civil War did Anthony, Stanton and Gage initiate the National Woman's Suffrage Association.

Delegates to the International Council of Women 1888. Seated: Second from right is Matilda Joslyn Gage; next to her is Elizabeth Cady Stanton. Second from left is Susan B. Anthony. *From the Library of Congress.*

Her Search for the Spiritual

It would be a mistake to assume Matilda was not religious because she criticized the institution of the church. (Wagner) Her rejection of the church was based on its patriarchal power and suppression of women. Gage maintained her membership in the Baptist church, but did not baptize her children. She looked for spiritual engagement outside the established church.

Matilda Joslyn Gage lived at a time when religion played a major role in the lives of the people in that central and western upstate region. It had been a hotbed of revivalism, known as a "burned over district," burned over by "the fiery spirit" of evangelical movements that coincided with and stimulated reform movements. (Goldsmith)

Gage was captivated by the philosophy, spirituality and practice of 19th century Spiritualism. Part of the wide appeal of Spiritualism was due to its embrace of the occult and practice of clairvoyance. The séance held out the hope of communication with the spirit of a loved one, especially one whose death was premature. Credibility for the séance may have been enhanced by Morse's invention of the telegraph, with its invisible means of communication. (Goldsmith)

With its promise of reincarnation, Spiritualism became a refuge, especially in the last years of Matilda's life. Spiritualism was socially respectable, attractive to middle and upper class women. Its popularity peaked at the end of the Civil War, with estimates of 10 million adherents. (Goldsmith)

Matilda used a séance to try to reach her grandchild Alice who had lived for only nine hours. (Mrs. Lincoln, too, sat in séances to contact the spirit of her dead son.) Eventually, the séance fell into disrepute because of fraudulent mediums.

Grandson Rob Baum remembered Matilda's letter explaining

that a person's spirit lives on after death and communicates with the living. Imagine the boy's fear of Grandma's ghost - her ashes were stored in the attic before being brought to Fayetteville for burial. (Loncraine)

Theosophy, a religious philosophy related to Spiritualism, became of greater interest in the closing years of Matilda's life. Theosophy embraced Eastern religious traditions and the ecumenical concept that all religions try to help humanity achieve the ideal of spiritual knowledge. Members of the Gage family read the works of Madame Blavatsky, the founder of the Theosophical movement. Gage had sent the Blavatsky book, *Isis Unveiled*, to all her children so they could exchange ideas despite their geographic distance. (Wagner)

Spiritualism, Theosophy, and Free Religion were similar in rejecting the confines of organized religion. Free Religionists chose reason to unite theology with science as a substitute for beliefs based on authority or tradition. Many adherents of Free Religion congregated in what were called "radical clubs" where they discussed theological questions and progressive ideas. And more! Matilda told her friend Martha Wright that she occasionally attended a Free Religionist club where women could freely discuss sexual concerns such as hygiene, abortion, eugenics and marriage. (Leach)

Like some contemporary feminists, Matilda thought about the Godhead as woman. She phrased it the "Divine Motherhood of God." Much to the discomfort of the women who attended the International Council of Women in Washington in 1888, Gage opened a meeting with a prayer to a female deity. Her prayer and speech did not go down well. The women there, in addition to the majority of suffragists, were devoted to a "masculine deity" and a religion that denied women any right to equality. (Kern) But the challenge Gage posed to the straight and narrow of that assembled group must have given her personal satisfaction, regardless of the women's discomfort.

Feminist: Both Passionate and Radical

*"The disenfranchisement of woman (has) let loose the reins
of violence which she only has the power to avert... All writers
recognize women as the great harmonizing elements..."*
                                    – Gage (Leach)

Matilda Joslyn Gage had been a very passionate woman.
Though Matilda looks rather formal and sedate in her photos,
her vociferous articles about the evils of patriarchy belie a "sedate"
woman. Gage never retreated from her radical theories and beliefs.

Exceptional intellect and passion are a potent mix. Matilda
had "fire in the belly." Passion gave her the courage to deliver
her maiden speech at the Syracuse Convention, despite her
inexperience and fear of public speechmaking. Passion fueled
her commitment to the First Amendment's guarantee of
separation of church and state. That principle permitted no
compromise when Anthony invited members of the Women's
Christian Temperance Union into the National Woman Suffrage
Association. To expand the movement was no excuse for
abandoning principle. Gage vented her outrage in a letter to her
son Thomas Clarkson with whom she corresponded regularly.

Even as Matilda lay dying, when fire in the belly would have
turned to embers, she wrote a speech for the commemoration of
the 50th anniversary of the Seneca Falls Convention.

How does one compare the quality of Gage's radicalism with
Stanton's? Stanton's Declaration of Sentiments at Seneca Falls
was certainly a radical document at the time. Stanton considered
herself a radical feminist. Her views of the church's responsibility
for the suppression of woman were the same as Gage's. However,
in the early days of the suffrage organization, she told Gage that
she preferred to postpone conflict with the church until after
their suffrage campaign was over.

Gage was responsible for the initiation of anti-church resolutions at NWSA conventions where she took every opportunity to educate, inform, and sometimes chastise women whom she thought were ignorant of the church's responsibility for woman's inferior status in society.

Stanton became more radical and angry at the church's subjugation of woman as she aged. In her book, *The Woman's Bible,* she charged that women's devotion to church and faith subjected them to "the very powers that made (woman's) emancipation impossible." (Kern) Stanton was denounced and ostracized by the religious and conservative women who dominated the merged suffrage organization, NAWSA, after her book was published in 1895. They called Stanton a "radical heretic."

Anthony was very much the moderate: in her thought, religious beliefs and action. She had strength of character, assertiveness, the power of independence. Anthony grew up in a Quaker home with a father who fostered the education of his daughters, free of gender discrimination. Another influence for moderation may have been her strict education at Deborah Moulson's Seminary, a reminder that every woman must strive for "morality, humility and piety." (Barry) Humility and piety are not a recipe for radical feminism.

Did the National Woman's Suffrage Association engage in the radical feminism of Stanton and Gage? Not really. NWSA activities were essentially mainstream, rather than radical, designed to gather public support. Advocacy consisted of meetings, public speeches, journal articles, petitions and annual conventions, especially petitions. Radical anti-church resolutions went down to defeat.

Petitions that gathered huge numbers of names were the favored attention-getting strategy. Annual conventions were held in Washington D.C. to address Congress and to lobby lawmakers, politely. During the 1879 Convention, Matilda Joslyn Gage, accompanied by several members, read a suffrage appeal to President Hayes.

NWSA took advantage of opportunities to place its cause front and center of the nation's attention. One such occasion was in Philadelphia, at the 1876 Centennial Celebration of America's Declaration of Independence. The women's request to participate in the official program had been rebuffed. Demanding to be heard, they designed an alternative strategy.

As soon as the original Declaration of 1776 had been read, Anthony, Gage and a few supporters marched up to the platform from which they had been excluded and handed the President of the Centennial Commission a three foot scroll containing the official "Woman's Declaration of Rights and Articles of Impeachment Against the Government of the United States." (Prominent are the signatures of Anthony, Gage and Stanton.)

The women's action appeared to be more theatrical than radical, a brief upset of the program's apple cart. Lucy Stone, though, lost no time criticizing the "sensational manner" in which Anthony and the women had acted. (DuBois, Correspondence) Copies of the Declaration were distributed to outstretched arms as the women marched to another platform in front of Independence Hall. There, Anthony read the NWSA Declaration, protected from the hot sun by Matilda's umbrella. In back of the women stood the old Liberty Bell.

The Declaration consisted of a laundry list of injustices. Women could not serve on juries, lacked the right to a fair trial, were taxed without representation and required to support war which they abhorred. Many states still deprived women of the right to own property, sue for divorce, or have custody of their children. Much was at stake besides the right to vote.

The women were particularly upset that the word "male" had been inserted for the very first time in the Constitution by the 14th Amendment giving former male slaves the right to vote. Gender had never before been written into the Constitution. Gender did not belong there now!

Economic injustices detailed in the Declaration were as important as the political. Women received lower wages for doing the same work as men. Women labored at home like slaves for no pay at all. "Women were arrested in disreputable houses while male partners went free … all on the pretense of regulating public morals."

There was no official government response. Criticism in the press more than compensated. Whether the women had truly engaged in radical behavior is a judgment better left to those who write history.

The "Woman's Declaration," now anointed by history, hangs in the room of the Vice-President in Washington. D.C.

Radical better describes the suffragists' protest at the dedication of the Statue of Liberty, ten years later in 1886. Angry that a woman was chosen to symbolize liberty, the protestors called the Statue the greatest hypocrisy of the 19th century. If that copper lady came down from her pedestal, she would not have the rights of a citizen in either America or France, they said. Although the women may have feigned some of their outrage, they were determined to lambaste the choice of a woman to represent Liberty when women were second class citizens. Matilda Joslyn Gage alone joined the New York City organization's demonstration. Neither Anthony nor Stanton was there.

Forewarned of the protest, organizers of the Statue of Liberty ceremony barred women from the dedication. Ladies were too "delicate" to withstand the crush of the crowd on that very small island in New York Harbor. The women decided to rent a boat. Could they afford it? President Lily Devereux Blake of the New York Suffrage Association requested approval of the expense from the organization's treasurer. The rental of a freight steamer would cost one dollar, one fourth of their total treasury!

While President Grover Cleveland and other male dignitaries pontificated at the ceremony, the steamer, packed with suffrage activists, the Governor of New Mexico and Lieutenant Governor of Wyoming circled the Island's festivities. Their message was carried by the only available technology of the day, a megaphone. Radical or not, the protest had been a savvy strategy.

Intellectual, Scholar and Theorist

Matilda Joslyn Gage and Elizabeth Cady Stanton were intellectuals, scholars, theorists, and exceptional writers. Anthony was intelligent and politically astute rather than intellectual, the engine of the women's reform movement. Gage was the movement's "chief historian and most thoughtful intellectual." She had "moved far beyond her old friends in matters of feminist theory." (Weatherford) Gage was "the most scholarly of all." (Flexner)

Intellect served ideology in designing political strategies. When Gage framed equal rights as human rights, she made the issue moral not merely political. Denial of human rights was an injustice, an obstacle to human progress. Gage believed the subjection of women was more immoral than the enslavement of Negroes because it…"sinks deeper into the national life, and upon it is built not only the physical well-being of the whole race of man, but the intellectual progress of humanity." (Leach)

In the 1870's, many suffrage movement leaders decided that there was no need for a suffrage law after all. Women were citizens. Citizens already had the right to vote under the Constitution! Government derived its just powers from the consent of the governed. Women were taxpayers and subject to all the laws of the land. Denial of the vote was taxation without representation and unconstitutional. Women were citizens. Instead, they were treated as subjects, denied the rights of citizenship and made inferior persons in the nation, in the home and in the workplace.

In a test case brought before the Supreme Court, Minor v. Happersett (1875) Virginia Minor charged she had been denied the vote by Happersett, the election official at her polling place in

Missouri. She sued Happersett for illegal deprivation of her right to vote. Minor asserted that as a citizen, her right to vote was guaranteed by the 14th Amendment. Not so. The Supreme Court ruled that citizenship did not automatically confer the right to vote. The decision was unanimous! Virginia Minor lost.

Exasperating inconsistencies were everywhere. Elections were under state jurisdiction, but Anthony was tried for voting illegally in a federal court. The federal government had granted suffrage to special groups of individuals, such as the former Civil War rebels and convicted felons, yet continued to refuse suffrage for women!

Liberty! Not for a married woman. She worked inside the home without a wage and worked outside the home for unequal pay. She had little protection under law from an abusive husband. What's more, there could be no liberty for a married woman without money of her own, without control over her own body and without the opportunities for independence. "Obedience to outside authority to which woman has everywhere been trained, has not only dwarfed her capacity, but made her a retarding force in civilization," Matilda wrote.

"Ideas that took (Gage) a lifetime to construct had to be recreated through a similar painstaking process by second wave feminist theorists." (Brammer)

PART III
LOOKING BACK
Femininity, Feminism and Sex

"Without the control of one's person, the opportunities of the world,
which are the only means of development, cannot be used."
— *Gage* (Leach)

Suffragists were disparaged by opponents and denigrated as
women lacking femininity. An Albany newspaper editor wrote,
"People are beginning to inquire how far public sentiment should
sanction or tolerate these unsexed women …frustrated old maids
…They scoff religion, repudiate the Bible and blaspheme God…"
(Smith)

Femininity at suffrage conventions would have given the lie to
the charge of "unsexed" women. They came dressed in rich silks,
laces, and the latest fashions. Gage had a "stylish wardrobe."
(Weatherford) Anthony was said to have patronized a "tip-top"
dressmaker in Rochester. "Walking and traveling dress" was not
merely a matter of fashion; dresses were indicators of social class.
(Leach)

Femininity, of course, is not to be confused with feminism. How
many suffragists were actually feminists? Not too many. The
word "feminist" in the 1870's would have distinguished a small
minority of women, those who wanted to transform women's
lives, not merely achieve the vote.

The meaning of the word "feminism" is somewhat elusive,
usually defined in the context of its time. "Feminism was not
a fixed ideology of equal rights"… (Leach) "The meaning of
feminism changes over time and in the hands of different

groups." (DuBois) A feminist, today, is still a woman who demands equality, but also one who identifies with women as a "class." (Barry) Feminist was not a label the majority of women welcomed then, or, for that matter, now.

Suffragists, women and men, were middle class. A minority of the population, they could afford the luxury of organization membership. For working class women, higher wages, better

Document of injustices afflicting women, written by Gage and Stanton for the Centennial of the Declaration of Independence, Philadelphia, 1876

working conditions and shorter hours were far more vital than the vote. Anthony, having been a teacher who was paid half the salary of male teachers, made considerable effort to enlist working women for the suffrage movement. She and Stanton started a Workingwoman's Association, but soon ran into organizational and financial problems. They were not oblivious to the significant education and social class differences between women in the workplace and their "sisters" in NWSA. None of those "sisters" had had any experience as wage laborers.

In fact, the large majority of women were anti-suffrage. Suffragists were a threat to family stability, to man's God-given superiority as father, husband and woman's protector; a threat to the status quo. Women were expected to conform to the all important virtues of piety, purity, submissiveness and homemaking, the "cult of domesticity." Unmarried women and women who defied "woman's sphere" were considered social deviants. Nonconformity in any age, especially for middle class women, poses a formidable challenge. And nonconformity could include a dangerous component: sex.

Modesty was a necessity, but women did know sexual desire. A woman who enjoyed sex too much put herself in a hazardous situation. She could have been given a medical diagnosis of "Female Neurasthenia." Neurasthenia was a female, not male, condition that included nervousness, hysteria or rebellious behavior. Remedies might have included a rest cure, confinement in a sanitarium, or in the extreme, a clitorodectomy. Although it may not have been frequent, surgical removal of the clitoris was justified as a way to quell neurasthenia and suppress sexual desire. (Goldsmith)

In a letter to a friend, Anthony criticized Stanton's seventh pregnancy with an implication of her sexuality. ..."for a moment's pleasure to herself or her husband (Mrs. Stanton) increased the load of care under which she already groans." (Goldsmith)

Birth control and its practices were criminalized under the Comstock law in 1873. It was illegal to mail or sell "obscene, lewd, lascivious" material, a description applied to any printed matter thought to be sexually provocative. It included information on contraceptives and physiology. A woman was arrested for selling a birth control manual at the Centennial celebration of the Declaration of Independence.

The Suffragists' Legacy

*"We are battling for those who shall come after us.
... they, not ourselves, shall enter into the harvest."*
— *Gage* (Wagner)

Feminist theorists in the 1980's revived the concepts Gage had developed in her writings. That …"patriarchy is a totalitarian regime… the dictatorship of the male" … that "men have denied women the knowledge of their own heritage" … and that "women are confined to cycles of lost and found, only to be lost and found again – and again." (Spender)

Passage of the Nineteenth Amendment in 1920 was too late for the three pioneers who died between 1898 and1906. Undoubtedly hard to accept, the triumvirate did foresee that suffrage would not be achieved in their lifetime. Reflecting upon her forty years of activism, Gage realized that victory would have to wait…"for those who shall come after us."

After Anthony's death, Carrie Chapman Catt, President of the merged NAWSA, redirected the movement. Suffrage campaigns were now focused on the states. Gone were the annual meetings in Washington to lobby for a Constitutional Amendment. The movement became more conservative and careful to preserve its white Anglo-Saxon character. NAWSA had turned its back on a Negro woman's request to censure discriminatory conditions for Pullman train porters. Anthony rationalized that suffragists were "helpless" to make a public statement. (Buhle) NAWSA had acted on its need to keep Southern members from leaving the suffrage movement.

That was not the first time that Anthony backed away from the issue of race. Ida B. Wells was turned down when she had requested permission for Negro women to form their own chapter of NWSA. (Ward and Burns) Anthony, a Quaker, would certainly have denied being a racist. She was a realist; she would not alienate the organization's Southern constituency, members who were less than steadfast in their commitment to the reform movement. The policy of ignoring racial prejudice continued long after Anthony was gone. Wells and her associates were told not to march with the Illinois delegation in the 1913 suffrage parade in Washington, D.C. (Ward and Burns) Egalitarian Matilda must have "turned over in her grave."

Not until 1912 did the national campaign for the vote come alive again. Only four states had granted women the vote: Wyoming, Utah, Colorado and Idaho. The radical suffragist Alice Paul (whose name disappeared from history for many years) took the women's movement into the streets. Nonviolent protests, for the first time, became a new strategy, one Matilda would have so greatly admired. Social change, Gage had written, required "rebellion."

Large scale, well-organized parades compelled the public's attention - parades that later figured as iconic photos in history textbooks. The women paraded the day before President Wilson's inauguration; the number estimated to include 10 to 20,000 marchers. By 1917, political confrontation had escalated. Alice Paul and her separate suffrage organization, the National Woman's Party, carried out a campaign of continuous picketing in front of the White House, a protest never before attempted. Posters compared President Wilson to the German Kaiser for his failure to support suffrage and democracy.

Suffragists, now called suffragettes, ridiculed and embarrassed Wilson. The women's tactics were nonviolent. But their demonstrations outside the White House provoked strong emotions. First they were arrested for obstructing traffic. Then their continued nonviolent protests provoked violence by soldiers and other men who were outraged by what they called the women's "disloyalty." The women, not the men, were arrested and imprisoned.

Shocking reports of the women's hunger strikes in prison were reported in the press. Brutal injuries women suffered from forced feedings hit the front pages. Their horrendous treatment aroused public sympathy, which no president could ignore for long. Wilson finally informed the Senate of his support for the Anthony Amendment.

Ratification of the Amendment required passage by three-fourths of the states. The struggle was not over. Southern states set up roadblocks to defeat the Amendment. Final passage in 1920 was a celebrated but exhausting victory. A woman's right to vote had taken 72 years of intense, tenacious, sometimes painful efforts. The women had mounted a grand total of 862 separate campaigns: in the states, in Congress, at political party conventions and at suffrage conventions. (Weatherford)

How are these suffrage pioneers perceived today? Each one of them was concerned about her personal legacy, sensitive to how she would be remembered in history. Anthony, who outlived Gage and Stanton, had the last word. She controlled the documents and facts that would shape the record of reform and her place in history. Stanton used her autobiography to project her persona and her life's work as she wished to be remembered. She also willed her brain to Cornell, sure of its special value for science research, but Stanton's brain was buried with her. Gage, who hoped that the liberation of women's lives from patriarchy would be her legacy, wrote her "magnum opus" *Woman, Church and State* for posterity.

An unanticipated legacy came from Matilda's son-In-law, L. Frank Baum, and his *Wizard of Oz* books. Baum had called his mother-in-law "one of the most remarkable women of her age." Maud's husband, Frank, was familiar with Matilda's writings on the ideals of justice and equality. He had undoubtedly read her book, *Woman, Church and State.*

Matilda came to live with the Baums the last two years of her life because she had become seriously ill. When she heard Frank tell his imaginative bedtime stories to his four young sons, she frequently urged him to publish the stories. (Wagner) Frank's utopian vision of society In the *Wizard of Oz* books was inspired by his mother-in-law. (Loncraine)
Ozma, the Princess of Oz, female ruler of the utopian Emerald

City reflects Matilda's feminist and egalitarian Ideology. There is no poverty, no cruel overseers, not a single evil person. All the residents are peaceful and kindhearted. Ozma refuses to fight invaders who are poised to conquer the City. She tells Dorothy, "No one has the right to destroy any living creatures, however evil they may be …" Dorothy's Aunt Em, faced with possible slavery by the invaders, is fearless. "I've been a slave all my life…" she said. (Baum) It was an echo of Gage's view that "…women are neither more nor less than SLAVES." (Wagner)

Gage's analysis of witchcraft and misogyny inspired the "storm conjuring witches" in the Land of Oz. (Wagner) Ever popular, Baum's books are a lasting tender tribute to his mother-In-law.

Anthony paid homage to Matilda Joslyn Gage in a condolence letter to Thomas Clarkson Gage. She praised his mother as "one of the most intensely earnest, true women we have ever had in our movement…Had she been possessed of a strong constitution…she would have done more for the emancipation of women than all the rest of us put together. With her feeble health, she accomplished wonders." (Notable American Women) Gage's feminist theories still resonate today. A woman's control over her own body, contraception, equal pay for equal work are insecure or unresolved. Patriarchy remains a power to be reckoned with.

PART IV
REFLECTIONS
On the Writing of History

Inadvertent errors sometimes creep into the writing of history and the historic record. A respected feminist historian, Alice Rossi, wrote that the president of the Akron, Ohio Suffrage Convention of 1851 was "noteworthy" because she was "the same woman who was later to edit the *History of Woman Suffrage.*" Rossi confused Frances Gage with Matilda. Frances Gage, In Ohio, was an abolitionist and suffrage activist, remembered for permitting ex-slave Sojourner Truth to speak at the Ohio suffrage convention. Frances Gage later recorded Sojourner Truth's speech from memory. The meeting in Ohio occurred a year before Gage attended her first woman's rights convention in Syracuse.

Eleanor Flexner wrote the first comprehensive history of the 19th century suffrage movement, published in 1959. *Century of Struggle,* has been widely used as a reference because it was the first modern account of the suffragists' movement. The book mentions Matilda Joslyn Gage only in passing, contributing to her invisibility. Flexner wrote that Gage was "tied for many years to a home and small children in an upstate New York town, (yet she) became the most scholarly of all." A second reference to Gage appeared in a footnote. Flexner noted that Gage was the only friend to help Anthony at the time of her trial. Her recognition of Matilda was so minimal, readers would have scarcely noticed.

Ellen DuBois, a prominent historian of the 19th century women's reform movement, makes the important point that "women's history was nonexistent before 1970."

The writing of history, or historiography, is inevitably Influenced by the historian's point of view, the time period in which he or she lived, his or her gender and prejudices too subtle to notice. For example, Samuel Eliot Morrison took the position that the prohibition movement was much more transformative than the women's equal rights movement.

Kathleen Barry, Susan B. Anthony's biographer, raised the issue of gender and challenged the dividing line between biography and history. "Women's biography must be a new reading of history...." Barry maintains that we can "discover what masculine history has suppressed ... from examining women's lives."

Elise Boulding, sociologist and author of *The Underside of History* (1992) criticized historiography for its gender prejudice. "There has been a massive injustice in the wholesale omission of women's contribution and participation in the histories of civilizations." Matilda Joslyn Gage criticized that same omission in her speech at the Syracuse Convention 140 years earlier.

Historian Sally Roesch Wagner published the first comprehensive work on Gage's life, *Matilda Joslyn Gage: She Who Holds the Sky* in 1998. In addition to writing several publications on Gage (see Bibliography) Wagner became the Executive Director of the Matilda Joslyn Gage Foundation which she founded in 2000. Established in Gage's former home in Fayetteville, the Foundation's mission is to educate, inform and inspire the continued pursuit of social justice – the mission to which Matilda Joslyn Gage dedicated her life.

Any substantial revision of nineteenth century suffrage history is not likely to happen. However, the proliferation of the media and internet make for greater opportunities to explore Gage, her feminist theories and contributions to literature. Perhaps Matilda Joslyn Gage will be personified someday in an historical novel like that of Marge Piercy's Sex Wars in which Anthony and Stanton are vividly brought to life.

One example of a recent revival of Matilda Joslyn Gage may be seen in the internet reference to Zanita Fenton. She presented a paper on Gage and *The Wonderful Wizard of Oz* at an Albany Law School Symposium in 2009. The paper analyzes the nature of power and hierarchy.

On Pursuing a Parent's Cause

It is curious that none of Matilda Joslyn Gage's children took up the cause their mother had so intensely pursued. Perhaps they experienced rivalry with Matilda's activism in NWSA and her dedication to writing. In addition, Gage's children may have found their mother's intellect so overwhelming that it inadvertently discouraged them from competing with her.

The Gage children, including son-in-law L. Frank Baum, greatly admired their mother's work. Matilda's son Thomas Clarkson appears to have been especially supportive of his mother and her work. Their frequent correspondence indicates he was her confidante.

The family did place great value on Matilda's papers and saved them. Several family members participated in the early work of establishing the Matilda Joslyn Gage Foundation. Granddaughter Matilda Jewell Gage generously contributed the papers she owned to the Gage Foundation.

In her famous speech, "Solitude of Self," Elizabeth Cady Stanton mused that reformers could not rely on their children to take up their cause and continue the work that dominated their mother's lives. However Harriot Stanton Blatch did enlist in her mother's cause, shaping it to her own vision and directing the outreach of the movement to working class and union women.

Jealous of Anthony's stardom in the suffrage constellation, Blatch made a concerted effort to restore her mother to historic prominence. She and her brother published their mother's correspondence, but Stanton's recognition and prominence had to wait. The very first biography of Elizabeth Cady Stanton by Alma Lutz was not published until 1940. The content, so much of which reproduces Stanton's writings, reflects Blatch's considerable assistance to Lutz.

Another of Stanton's daughters, Margaret Stanton Lawrence, described the rivalry she and her siblings experienced from the *History of Woman Suffrage,* which occupied so much of their mother's time. The *History* was like "some favorite adopted child that filled (our) places in a mother's heart." (Gordon, Vol. IV Appendix)

On Feminism

Feminist issues are usually tied to the political and economic climate in which women's demands for social change are asserted. A recent feminist concern is the assumption that women can "have it ALL." Can a woman manage a high-powered career and simultaneously care for her children's health, encourage their school success, attend their soccer games and emerge with her self and her professional position still whole?

Male standards, Gage might write today, still predominate in the workplace with few exceptions. Women, especially those in executive corporate positions, are usually expected to adhere to traditional, male-established patterns that can conflict with their lives as mothers and wives. Family pressures for fathers and husbands are still not equivalent. Although there are family friendly workplaces, significant changes are still a work in progress.

Similarities between women who fought for equal employment rights In the 19th century and women who fight to make the workplace a level playing field for women and men today are apparent. Pay inequity stubbornly persists. Women, on average, earn 77 cents to a man's dollar. And sexual harassment, subtle or flagrant, continues to be a challenge to a woman's integrity, job retention and/or career advancement.

Women, many who would not identify themselves as feminists, are up against the barricades again fighting for control over their own bodies, the preservation of Roe v. Wade and health care insurance that includes birth control independent of the employer's religious convictions.

On Advocacy and its Unintended Consequences

Susan B. Anthony, the icon for woman's right to vote, earned primacy through her strong leadership and expansion of the suffrage movement. Anthony still overshadows Elizabeth Cady Stanton and obscures Matilda Joslyn Gage with the general public.

Not to depreciate Anthony – her success was also responsible for the movement's failure at the end, something she did not anticipate nor intend. The women's cherished vote failed to promote their equality in either government or the church. When Anthony rejected the political goals advocated by Stanton and Gage, achievement of the vote left no equal rights platform around which the women could rally. The vote in itself would not and did not free women from their unequal status in American culture and government.

Anthony had given complete priority to advocacy for the vote in order to avoid conflict and division in their organization. Unity among the diverse membership required that there be only one issue.

Gage and Stanton's impassioned efforts for woman's emancipation became part of forgotten history; their writings collected dust.

With the passage of the 19th Amendment, the National American Woman's Suffrage Association transformed itself into the nonpartisan League of Women Voters, dedicated to education for informed participation in elections and government, not woman's equal rights.

The movement's failure gave birth to the campaign for the Equal Rights Amendment, four decades later. But ERA failed to achieve passage by three-fourths of the states.

Women's equal rights are still being fought for – one at a time.

BIBLIOGRAPHY

Introduction

The search for Matilda Joslyn Gage's recognition and inclusion in history included fifty books and internet references. They are reviewed in this bibliography with copyright dates, not publishers, to trace and identify Gage's emergence in history. Histories of the 19th century woman's equal rights reform movement did not recognize Matilda Joslyn Gage as one of its three prominent leaders until 1998. If Gage could be found in a history or biography published prior to 1980, she would be mentioned only in passing or in a footnote...with one exception.

The earliest reference to Gage, published in her lifetime in 1893, is A *WOMAN OF THE CENTURY: 1470 Biographical Sketches Accompanied by Portraits of Leading American Women in All Walks of Life,"* edited by Willard and Livermore. Mary Livermore was a suffragist who knew Matilda Joslyn Gage.

Gage's prominence as a suffrage leader, theorist and feminist first appeared in *MATILDA JOSLYN GAGE: She Who Holds the Sky* by historian Sally Roesch Wagner in 1998. Wagner is the Founder and Executive Director of the Matilda Joslyn Gage Foundation and Museum in Fayetteville, New York. (See link under Internet References.)

Excluded from Suffrage History by Leila Brammer, published in 2000, focuses on the reasons for Gage's omission from history. *True Love and Perfect Union* by William Leach recognized Gage's stature as a feminist theorist, giving her visibility in more than a passing reference. Published in 1980, Leach's book was the first to recognize Gage in the 20th century.

The University of Connecticut and Connecticut State Library Systems proved to have very fine collections for a modest explorer of history. Although *The Search for Matilda* concentrated on print publications, several internet links to Gage references are included and listed at the end of the Bibliography.

Banner, Lois W. *ELIZABETH CADY STANTON: A Radical for Women's Rights* c. 1980
Banner includes recognition of Gage as the "only suffragist of record" to use the history of women's accomplishments as proof that women deserve the same rights as men. Gage's work as a feminist theorist and interpreter of history foretold contemporary feminist thought.

Barry, Kathleen, *SUSAN B. ANTHONY* c. 1988
Gage is in the Index for a total of 15 pages. Story of Gage holding an umbrella to protect Anthony from the sun at the 1876 Centennial of the Declaration of Independence is here. Gage confronted gender discrimination there when she tried to rent an office for NWSA. in Philadelphia for the 1876 Centennial. A married woman's signature was unacceptable; Anthony had to sign the contract.

Anthony trusted Gage. She confided in her when Stanton provoked her anger for supporting Woodhull against her wishes. Anthony wrote that Gage believed she was being overshadowed and given insufficient loyalty, an observation that was validated when Anthony took advantage of Gage's unavoidable absence to merge two competing suffrage organizations.

The merger posed a threat to separation of church and state and important policy strategies. Gage organized and opened the first meeting of her Woman's National Liberal Union one week after the first meeting of the merged suffrage associations.

Brammer, Leila, *EXCLUDED FROM SUFFRAGE HISTORY: Matilda Joslyn Gage 19th Century American Feminist* ©2000
Brammer's research and analysis of Gage's exclusion from the history of the suffrage movement was originally part of her PH.D. thesis. She clarifies Gage's contributions to the reform movement as scholar, activist and feminist theorist.

Book describes Gage's theory of patriarchy and its control over church and state, the church's suppression of woman, and the double standard for men and women in the law and its enforcement.

Gage was more egalitarian than Stanton or Anthony; she advocated for poor women, exposed unequal pay and the injustice of woman's unpaid labor at home.

Anthony feared subversion of the suffrage movement from Gage's and Stanton's criticism of church. Gage opened session of International Council of Women in 1888 with prayer to female deity. She was devoted to Spiritualism later in life. Brammer states Gage's "exclusion was not personal but the result of complex political process that pushed the issues she thought important to the sidelines." Maintains Gage's exclusion from history was a political consequence of her controversial, radical positions.

Gage's departure from suffrage activity came after the merger of the two suffrage organizations. Gage accused Anthony of betrayal. She reacted by organizing Woman's National Liberal Union. Gage and Stanton, no longer active in the movement after1890, "extinguished the core of the 19th century movement." Gage's "thought was far ahead of her time" and "remarkably applicable to the present." Loss of her work "was a loss for all women."

Buhle, Mari Jo & Buhle, Paul, C *ONCISE HISTORY OF WOMAN SUFFRAGE Selections from History of Woman Suffrage and National American Woman Suffrage Association* ©2005

Collection of original suffrage writings with editorial commentaries. Suffrage movement represents "little understood but vital phase of American reform." States importance of petition campaigns. Cites NAWSA rejection of black woman's request to address conditions for Pullman train workers. (1899) Source of many Gage quotes: "Obedience to outside authority …

made (women) a retarding force in civilization…" Women were victims of fanaticism in history. Women's labor was exploited: "Woman has been the great unpaid laborer of the world…" "The two great sources of progress are intellect and wealth. Education frees the mind from the bondage of authority…" Gage placed woman's rights movement within history of Western civilization. She researched and documented women's intellectual achievements and inventions throughout civilization, citing women whose names are little known.

As a feminist, Gage distrusted male-dominated reform; thought men's recognition of women's contributions to the support of the Civil War was inadequate.

DuBois, Ellen Carol, *FEMINISM AND SUFFRAGE: The Emergence of an Independent Women's Movement* ©1848-1869. ©1978
Gage was not included in this book. (Note copyright date.) DuBois emphasizes suffragism as a social movement and its relevance for the history of feminism as a movement for "radical change" in women's lives. Describes origin of Anthony/Stanton friendship and suffragists' middle class perspective.

DuBois, Ellen Carol, *ELIZABETH CADY STANTON / SUSAN B. ANTHONY CORRESPONDENCE, WRITINGS, SPEECHES* © 1981 and 1984
Only three Gage references in the selected correspondence in this collection. First is a memo written by Gage, Stanton and Hooker regarding cooperation with Victoria Woodhull. Anthony rejected cooperation with Woodhull. Second is a reference to Gage's opposition to merger with AWSA which motivated her to organize Woman's National Liberal Union in 1890. Third is the divergence among the three leaders in the1880's:Anthony to strengthen the organization's network, and Gage and Stanton to concentrate on feminist issues and goals.

NWSA petitioned Congress for woman suffrage for the first time in 1885.

DuBois, Ellen Carol, *HARRIOT STANTON BLATCH AND THE WINNING OF WOMAN SUFFRAGE* ©1997
Hostility between Susan B. Anthony and Lucy Stone resulted in Stone's omission from Volume II of *History of Woman Suffrage* which covered the late1860's. Opposing factions split the suffrage movement into two organizations: National Woman's Suffrage Association (NWSA) and American Woman's Suffrage Association (AWSA). Stanton's daughter, Harriot Stanton Blatch wrote the final chapter of Vol. II of *History of Woman Suffrage* in order to rectify AWSA's omission.

Blatch, whose husband was English, lived in England for many years and was greatly influenced by the English reform campaigns of 1880's and 1890's. She recognized the changed conditions and impact of social class on the American suffrage movement. Believed suffrage could never become a mass movement until it included working women. "Suffragette" was a pejorative name to describe a militant woman who engaged in parades, demonstrations, and open air speeches.

DuBois, Ellen Carol, *WOMAN SUFFRAGE AND WOMEN'S RIGHTS* ©1998
Gage wrote supplementary essays on histories of women in the *American Revolution, Christian misogyny and witchcraft for the History of Woman Suffrage*. DuBois states that historiography of women's history is "nonexistent before 1970." States that histories of women's equal rights reform efforts, written during 1920's, '30's and '40's, were not "professional." Not academic histories, they were written for popular consumption.
"Feminism" as a word came into existence around 1910.
Suffrage militants challenged existing standards of femininity.

Flexner, Eleanor, *CENTURY OF STRUGGLE* ©1959; 1975
Flexner wrote the first modern history of the 19th century woman's equal rights reform movement. She was not an academic historian. Gage appears only twice in its 375 pages. Gage was "tied for many years to home and small children in

upstate NY town…but became the most scholarly of all." The second reference to Gage describes her assistance to Anthony before her trial for voting illegally. She delivered public speeches in 16 Ontario County Districts while Anthony spoke in 21. Flexner credits Gage as the only friend and co-worker to come to Anthony's aid in a footnote.

Gage, Matilda Joslyn, WOMAN, CHURCH AND STATE ©1893 and 2002
Introduction by Sally Roesch Wagner provides overview of Gage's historic importance to 19th century women's reform movement and highlights her special contributions as a radical feminist. Gage spent last eight years of her life "estranged from most of her movement allies and friends of the previous 40 years."

Gage's brief introduction to *Woman, Church and State* expresses her indignation at the institutionalized injustices committed as a consequence of patriarchy over Church and State. Written originally as a 40 page chapter in *History of Woman Suffrage*, it was later expanded into the book, *Woman, Church and State*, to integrate and report more of the details of her "investigation over 20 years."

Gage called *Woman Church and State* her "magnum opus." It is not only a history but an impressive analysis of cultural and social issues we identify today as anthropology, sociology, psychology and economics. Gage's writing is interdisciplinary (a nonexistent term at that time).

Gage describes matriarchies that existed prior to Christianity. Chapters are devoted to feudalism, the misogyny of witchcraft, celibacy and its ramifications for marriage, and patriarchy's domination over society and culture. Gage believed that the church's enormous power over marriage, education, property and work enabled it to suppress and subjugate women.

The church taught that woman was created inferior to man, created for man and was first in sin. That as soon as a woman departs from her traditional sphere, she becomes atheistic and immoral, thus the ban on woman's voice being heard in public. "Society has everywhere been permeated with disregard for woman's rights of person."

Gage's ability to combine the erudite research required to write *Woman, Church and State,* with her political activism and dedication to family boggles the mind.

Gage's book, printed by a socialist publisher, was banned from the Fayetteville Library because of Comstock who threatened to arrest school board members if they put the book in school libraries. Gage's book stayed in print from 1893 until 1917. The book was admired by Tolstoy and Woodhull.

Gage, Matilda Joslyn, *WOMAN, CHURCH AND STATE* ©1980 (earlier edition)
The 1980 edition of this book has a provocative subtitle: *"The Original Expose of Male Collaboration Against the Female Sex"* and a Foreword written by Mary Daly. Daly was a radical feminist philosopher, academic and theologian who described herself as a "radical feminist lesbian." She refused to let men attend her classes in Boston College.

Daly wrote: "I'm concerned with women's capacities, which have been infinitely diminished under patriarchy," an echo of Matilda's cry. Even more radical, Daly argues against equality of the sexes..."women ought to govern men."

Introduction by Sally Roesch Wagner here is nine pages longer than her fifteen page introduction to the 2002 edition. Wagner's overview of the history of the movement and the suffrage triumvirate who led the movement frame Gage's contributions. In 1980, Wagner wrote that the main reason for Gage's exclusion from history was due to Anthony's merger of the two suffrage organizations.

Ginzberg, Lori, *ELIZABETH CADY STANTON* ©2009
Gage distributed NWSA literature at 1876 Centennial that decried the "one discordant note" in a nation "buoyant with

patriotism." *New York Tribune* reported NWSA's challenge to the Centennial Program as a "discourteous interruption."

Quotes Stanton who wrote that Gage "had a knack of rummaging through old libraries, bringing more startling facts to light than any woman I ever knew." In a footnote, she writes: Anthony occasionally pleaded with Gage to "scan the law and the logic" of a Stanton position she considered absurd..."if she and you see the matter alike - I shall surrender." (Anthony letter to Gage, Apr. 27 1886.)

Stanton presented herself as "harmless, benign and motherly," but Ginzberg calls her "radical, arrogant, heretical, self-centered, elitist, stubborn, uncompromising, smug." ..."Younger women admired Anthony not Stanton." They gave Anthony gifts of money, jewels, and silks.

Stanton had willed her brain to Cornell, but she was buried with her brain in tact.

By 1894, suffrage had become a popular position, a "fashionable fad" according to Ginzberg. Her list of "reform luminaries" includes Grimke sisters, Lucretia Mott, and Lucy Stone; omits Gage! Yet the book's bibliography includes Gage's *Woman, Church and State.*

Goldsmith, Barbara, *OTHER POWERS: The Age of Suffrage, Spiritualism and the Scandalous Victoria Woodhull* ©1998 "Spiritualism and the inception of women's rights were intertwined." The séance coincided with Morse's invention of the telegraph.

Edward Bayard, Stanton's brother-in-law and Stanton practiced homeopathy, considered quackery by the establishment. Neurasthenia, a term for nervousness and hysteria, was a condition attributed only to females - associated with woman's sexual drive at that time. Rest cure or even clitoridectomy were used to quell sexual desire. (1868)

Goldsmith describes Anthony Comstock's crusade against vice and pornography.

When Stanton became pregnant with child #7, Anthony wrote to a friend: "for a moment's pleasure to herself or her husband, she should thus increase the load of care under which she already groans..."

Stanton was an Independent candidate in NY's 8th Congressional District in 1866 and won 24 (male) votes. Although women couldn't vote, they could serve if elected. Book has significant content on suffrage, Stanton and Anthony, but nothing on Gage.

Gordon, Ann D. editor, *SELECTED PAPERS OF ELIZABETH CADY STANTON & SUSAN B. ANTHONY,* Volumes I, II, III, IV and V, Rutgers University Press, ©1997
This enormous research project began in 1982. Volume VI was issued in 2012. Documents collected were located in more than 200 libraries in the U.S., Canada, England, New Zealand, Netherlands, France, and Germany. Sources include newspapers, periodicals and correspondence.

Why was Gage omitted from this project? Was it a consequence of Gage's invisibility in 1982 when the scope of the project was designed? This enormous work was reviewed only to search for any correspondence with Gage. There are only a total of eleven letters to or from Gage in the five volumes of almost 5,000 pages. Letters of interest: Anthony rejected Gage's request for an NWSA resolution to oppose amnesty for Confederate leaders to restore their political rights. Anthony insisted NWSA focus only on woman suffrage and not put the organization in opposition to any efforts at vote restoration. (1875) Vol. III

Stanton letter to Gage urged an NWSA resolution that would require education to be compulsory for citizenship and the vote. (1877) Vol. III.

Gage submitted a bill for $168 to NWSA for reimbursement of her expenditures. (Vol. IV)

Stanton's daughter Margaret (1885) described the scene where Anthony and Stanton worked and how they handled and resolved disputes. "Susan punctilious on dates, mother on philosophy." Stanton's children felt the History was like "some favorite adopted child that filled their places in a mother's heart." (Article by Margaret Stanton Lawrence in Appendix of Vol. IV.) Gordon quotes letter of complaint from Gage to Lillie Devereux Blake, (March 1891) "It has always been the policy of Susan & Stanton to play into each other's hands and to hold each other up at the expense of all other workers." (Introduction to Vol. V)

Griffin, Lynne and McCann, Kelly, *THE BOOK OF WOMEN: 300 Notable Women History Passed By* ©1992
Gage not included. Listed among the women suffrage history passed by were: Abby and Julia Smith, Alice Paul, Lucy Burns, Pankhurst sisters, Anna Shaw, Lydia Child, Mary Livermore. Other notable women that history passed by: Catherine L. Greene (cotton gin) Lucy Stone (kept maiden name) Fanny Wright (abolitionist) Anna Ella Carroll (author of Union's Tennessee campaign) Rose Schneiderman (labor) Florence Kelley (social reformer).

Griffith, Elisabeth, *IN HER OWN RIGHT: The Life of Elizabeth Cady Stanton* ©1984
Anthony had to send Gage to urge Stanton to come to July 1776 Centennial – she arrived late in June. Partnership agreement to produce *History of Woman Suffrage* specified all three names would appear on title page, share copyright and divide the profits. Griffith states that Gage was brought into History project "as a buffer."

Gage sat on Executive Committee of American Equal Rights Association (which preceded NWSA).

Gage's work on History cut short by Henry's illness and her need to manage his store, but she continued to work at home. "True womanhood" defined woman as "domestic, maternal, religious, cultured and subservient."

Anthony and Gage endorsed Grant not Woodhull for President. Stanton also opposed merger of NWSA and AWSA. She supported Gage's plan to organize an alternative association with broader platform, but her support was only verbal, it never materialized.

Kern, Kathi, *MRS. STANTON'S BIBLE,* c. 2001
Kern examines what she identifies as the "missing piece of the historiographical record" of the suffrage movement," particularly the last decade of the 19th century in which religion dominated the dialogue and conflicts generated by the radical anti-church, anti-clerical feminists, Elizabeth Cady Stanton and Matilda Joslyn Gage.

Religion played a "pivotal role …in the transformation of the direction, leadership and ideology of the 19th century suffrage movement."

Both Stanton's *Woman's Bible* and Gage's *Woman, Church and State* were denounced by the second generation suffragists who had taken over the leadership of the movement.

There are important references to Gage which confirm the rivalry, tensions and competition between Gage and Stanton. There were quarrels over Stanton's use of Gage's motto without attribution in her autographs, the failure to include Gage in the copyright of the *Woman's Bible* as had been agreed upon, and Gage's fear that Stanton was appropriating her original work, or "stealing her thunder" on the history of Matriarchates. Describes Gage at Women's International Council who made a speech on the "Divine Motherhood of God."

The two women were "secularists," joined in their great interest in Theosophy. …" the battles of late 19th century were waged between evangelicals and secularists."

Stanton wrote that women were the chief support of the church and clergy to their own detriment because church and clergy were "the very powers that made her emancipation impossible." Stanton's book fueled the concerted, and soon successful, effort to exclude Stanton's name from the suffrage movement. The book was revived (18 years later) as a tool to defeat ratification of the 19th Amendment.

Leach, William, *TRUE LOVE AND PERFECT UNION: Feminist Reform of Sex and Society* ©1980
Index references Gage in 27 pages. Published in 1980, this was the only book that included significant content about Gage prior to 1998 when Wagner published her monograph on Gage, *She Who Holds the Sky.*

Leaders of suffrage movement were foremothers of 20th century feminists. They demanded autonomy, equal legal and social status with husbands, equal pay, property rights, and a woman's control over her own body. Reform efforts included divorce from an abusive husband; access to professions and higher education. Equal rights, more than suffrage, dominated the women's writings. Many equal rights issues were the same as those in the women's movement 100 years later.

"Feminism was not a fixed ideology of equal rights, but a multi-faceted egalitarian ideology determined and limited by its historical matrix."

Gage was a feminist historian who studied the past to find women inventors and innovators. She found women who invented embroidery, the cotton gin, pillow lace, the straw bonnet, bread and the science of medicine.

Gage, Anthony and Stanton all supported federal (as opposed to state) legislation to secure women's rights... believed that "in the concentration of national power (lies) the basic prerequisite for the expansion of human freedom."

Gage quotes: "Without the control of one's person, the

opportunities of the world, which are the only means of development, cannot be used." She considered women the great harmonizing influence…"the movement for the enfranchisement of women is the movement for universal humanity (which will) weld together all the interests of the human family." "The present disorganization of society warns us that in the disenfranchisement of woman we have let loose the reins of violence and ruin which she only has the power to avert…." Stanton wrote, "The male element ….overpowered the feminine element everywhere, until we know little of true manhood and womanhood."

Gage objected to men chairing women's rights societies because "women could work more successfully for their own freedom than anyone else can work for them." She did include men as vice-presidents in the New York State Suffrage Association. Gage believed that the subjection of woman was a deeper moral question than slavery because it…"sinks deeper into the national life, and upon it is built not only the physical well-being of the whole race of man, but the intellectual progress of humanity." Leach describes Gage's great interest in Spiritualist movement. Free Religionists and "radical clubs" gave women the opportunity to discuss issues relating to sex.

Feminists were not without interest in fashion. Anthony patronized "tip-top" dressmaker in Rochester. Feminists went to conventions dressed in "rich and elegant silks… laces…cut in the latest fashions."

Leach describes feminist reformers' interest and participation in social sciences, Utopian Socialism and civic organizations. Utopian socialists established a set of ideals as an alternative to capitalism, such as Robert Owen's New Harmony. Bellamy's book, *Looking Backwards,* made socialism acceptable to the middle class.

States that Comte and Positivism influenced Stanton's philosophy and thought.

Loncraine, Rebecca, *THE REAL WIZARD OF OZ:*
The Life and Times of L. Frank Baum ©2009
This biography of L. Frank Baum includes his mother-in-law, Matilda Joslyn Gage, his admiration for her and their relationship.

Baum and the Gage family distanced themselves from orthodox Christianity. Gage refused to have any of her children baptized. Gage and Baum were admirers of Theosophy; shared an interest in Spiritualism and the occult. Held séances in Aberdeen to contact Gage's granddaughter. Rob Baum was fearful of grandmother's ghost because Gage's ashes were up in attic.

Gage described as complex, unpredictable, impulsive person. Loncraine highlights content of Gage's Woman, Church and State, a book admired by Tolstoy and Woodhull.
Gage adopted into Wolf Clan of the Mohawk Nation.

Anthony visited Baum family and Gage when traveling thru Dakota to campaign for suffrage amendment. Baum was Secretary of Aberdeen's Equal Suffrage Club: membership 34 women, 36 men.

Bibliography includes: *In Other Lands Than Ours* a privately published work by Maud Gage Baum, 1907 and *"L. Frank Baum: An Inside Introduction to the Public"* by Helen Leslie Gage in The Dakotan 1903. Neither of these writings could be found.

Lunardini, Christine, *WHAT EVERY AMERICAN SHOULD KNOW ABOUT WOMEN'S HISTORY* ©1994
A chronological collection of short essays highlighting important events and people for women in American History. The only reference to Gage here is as one of the three editors of *History of Woman Suffrage.*

19th century: The short essays that refer to suffrage and women's equal rights include: 1848 Seneca Falls Convention; initiation of NWSA and AWSA; Minor v. Happerset Supreme Court Decision; *Woman Suffrage Amendment (*written by Stanton) first submitted to Congress in 1878. Merger of NWSA and AWSA in 1890; Alice Paul leads protest at Wilson's inauguration in 1913; Ida Husted Harper edits final two volumes of *History of Woman Suffrage* in 1922.

20th century: Essays include the Civil Rights Act that prohibits sex discrimination in employment,1964; Title IX that bans sex discrimination in federally funded education programs,1972; Congress passes Equal Rights Amendment (originally written by Alice Paul in 1923). ERA failed passage by three-fourths of the states.

Lutz, Alma, *CREATED EQUAL: A BIOGRAPHY OF ELIZABETH CADY STANTON* ©1940
This first biography of Elizabeth Cady Stanton consists mostly of quoted excerpts from Stanton's correspondence and writings. Harriot Stanton Blatch's contribution is evident.
There are references to Gage in 19 pages. She is described as one of ten "best known writers" for the Equal Rights Association newspaper, "Revolution." Her articles covered issues of equal pay for equal work, eight hour workday, educated suffrage, abolition of standing armies.

The Equal Rights Association was dominated by men and supported the 15th amendment which failed to include vote for women. Women's anger over ERA support of the Amendment without the vote for women caused a permanent rift and the initiation of the National Woman Suffrage Association.

Lutz refers to Gage's assistance to Anthony before her trial and to shading Anthony with umbrella at 1876 Centennial. Stanton initiated 16th Amendment for woman suffrage; introduced in Congress in 1869.

Three suffrage leaders started writing the History in 1876. Their agreement: Stanton and Gage would do the writing, Anthony would get it published and the three women would share profits. Stanton lectured for the Lyceum Bureau for 12 years, 8 months a year, from 1869-1881. Earned $3-4000 a year to help pay for her children's college tuitions. Stanton discussed collaboration with several women including Gage to work on *The Woman's Bible*. Gage was never credited with her collaboration on Volume II of *The Woman's Bible*.

Norgren, Jill, B*ELVA LOCKWOOD:The Woman Who Would be President* ©2007
There are many references to Gage, Anthony and Stanton because Lockwood, a pioneering attorney, was an activist in the suffrage movement and a friend of Gage's. Lockwood had been a good friend of Anthony's in the 1850's before conflicts resulted in Anthony's animosity towards her years later.

Gage and Lockwood were friends for 15 years. She supported Lockwood's campaign for president in 1884 and became an elector-at-large. Anthony and Stanton did not support Lockwood's candidacy. Believing it no longer served an educational purpose, Gage did not support Lockwood's second campaign for president in 1888.

When Anthony purposely omitted Lockwood from the program of the International Council of Women's meeting, Gage wrote to a friend that Anthony could be very harsh to someone she "hates."

Lockwood, a Methodist, liked Willard and was more conservative than Gage, yet she attended the first meeting of Gage's WNLU organization in 1890. In 1888, only three states had suffrage: Utah, Wyoming and Washington. Women could vote for school boards in 14 states.

O'Neill, William, *EVERYONE WAS BRAVE: The Rise and Fall of Feminism in America* © 1969
Preface explains that book is inquiry into "failure of feminism" i.e. suffrage did not succeed in changing the lives of women.

The feminist movement failed to recognize "the limits that the organization of society placed upon its larger aspirations." "...feminism resulted from the emergence of the nuclear family." Only one page refers to Gage. She testified to a NY State Senate Committee disputing the Committee's contention that women should not be given the vote until they were "fit" for it. Stanton was called an "elitist" ...her "assault on Christian Doctrine" was capped by her book, *The Woman's Bible*.

Anthony believed economic power would follow political power. ..."a disenfranchised class is always an oppressed class." Thought the vote for women would secure equal pay for equal work. A former teacher, she had received half the salary of her male colleagues.

Women reformers who figure prominently in this book are Elizabeth Cady Stanton (23 pages) Carrie Chapman Catt (27 pages) Jane Addams (31 pages) and Florence Kelley (30 pages).

Piercy, Marge. *SEX WARS* ©2006
Found this historical novel listed under "suffrage" in the library's internet catalog. The novel has four major characters: Elizabeth Cady Stanton, Victoria Woodhull, Anthony Comstock and one fictional character, a Jewish immigrant woman. Their lives are skillfully interwoven in their historical period.

Matilda Joslyn Gage appears briefly as Stanton's friend, co-editor, and co-author of the women's Declaration of Independence at the 1876 Centennial in Philadelphia.

Stanton's admiration for Woodhull's fierce determination to be an independent woman is more nonfiction than fiction in this novel. Woodhull exercised her freedom both as a business woman and as a woman free to follow her sexual desires.

Woodhull's efforts to control the 1872 NWSA Convention for the benefit of her political campaign for the presidency caused a blow-up between Stanton and Anthony – more intense in the novel it seemed than in history. Woodhull met her match when Anthony prevented Woodhull from continuing her speech and takeover of the NWSA Convention's platform. Anthony extinguished the lights in the meeting hall. (Fact, not fiction.) Anthony Comstock, a one man crusader to enforce the laws against pornography and obscenity, figures prominently in this novel as he wages an anti-vice campaign, ensnares free love practitioner Victoria Woodhull and puts her in jail.

Rivette, Barbara S. *FAYETTEVILLE'S FIRST WOMAN VOTER* ©1969 and 2006
Short biography of Matilda Joslyn Gage. This work grew out of the Fayetteville-Manlius League of Women Voters celebration of the 50th anniversary of the 19th Amendment. In addition to a fifteen page biography of Gage, the booklet describes Gage's success in getting woman suffrage in New York State school elections.

Rossi, Alice, *THE FEMINIST PAPERS* ©1973
This is a history of feminism with excerpts from historic writings. Describes Akron, Ohio Suffrage Convention, 1851, as "noteworthy" because the president, Frances Gage was "the same woman who was later to edit the *History of Woman Suffrage* with Stanton and Anthony..." an unfortunate error.
"She (Gage) was a scholarly and dedicated woman, with perhaps the best ability for historical research to assure accuracy and to ferret out details in the preparation of the *History*"... a description of Matilda not Frances!

Includes an excerpt from an article in the *History of Woman Suffrage*, *"Political Equality for Women."* It reads "Women have led armies in all ages, have held positions in the army and navy for years in disguise..." The article is unsigned but has the earmarks of Matilda's knowledge of history.

Sherr, Lynn and Kazickas, Jurata, *SUSAN B. ANTHONY SLEPT HERE: A Guide to American Women's Landmarks.* ©1976 and 1994

Book describes and illustrates important landmarks of famous women. Entries are organized by state and cities within each state. Index of names is the key to finding a geographic site for any famous woman. Included are Gage's grave and house in Fayetteville, New York.

Stanton's house in Tenafly, New Jersey, is identified as the place where cartons of letters and documents were shipped for inclusion in *History of Woman Suffrage.*

Smith, Page, *DAUGHTERS OF THE PROMISED LAND, WOMEN IN AMERICAN HISTORY* ©1970
Editor of the Albany Register wrote (after New York Women's Rights Convention): "People are beginning to inquire how far public sentiment should sanction or tolerate these unsexed women, who make a scoff of religion, who repudiate the Bible and blaspheme God: who would step out from the true sphere of the mother, the wife and the daughter…and overturn all the social relations of life."

States that hundreds of thousands of women supported emancipation of the slave. Anti-slavery "cadres" of women became activists for woman's rights movement.

Spender, Dale ed. *FEMINIST THEORISTS: Three Centuries of Key Women Thinkers* ©1983
Essay on Gage is by Lynne Spender. Includes many Gage quotes: "men rob women of their labor, all their labor – physical, emotional and intellectual." The organizations of church and state were "devised by men in order to preserve their power." Gage wrote that men denied women's contributions or robbed them for themselves.
Other Gage quotes include: …"patriarchy is a totalitarian regime. It is the dictatorship of the male." …"men have denied women the knowledge of their own heritage." "…women are confined to cycles of lost and found, only to be lost and found again – and again."

Stansell, Christine, *CITY OF WOMEN: Sex and Class in New York,* ©1789-1860. 1982, 1986
Upper and middle class women saw themselves as "moral guardians of families and nation" which perhaps compensated them for the freedom they were denied. Explains position of anti-suffragists.

Middle class women's views about working class women were abstract. Anthony became better informed about working women's lives in the 1870's when she tried to organize them to support suffrage. Working women's different goals and social class made for lack of success in Anthony's and Stanton's efforts to organize them for suffrage.

Stanton, Elizabeth Cady, *EIGHTY YEARS AND MORE: Reminiscences,* 1815-1897 ©1898, re-issued 1993
Part personal reminiscences, part history, part political philosophy, and Stanton's feminist ideology constitute this autobiography. Stanton recreates the time, her society and the many barriers in the struggle for women's equal rights. She describes the opposition she faced particularly on her advocacy for divorce, for women to fill church offices, as well as for suffrage.

Stanton and Gage both tried to "rouse" women to their degraded position in the Church.

Stanton's dedication to Susan B. Anthony reads, "My steadfast friend for half a century."

Gage is included in comments about the 1876 Centennial in Philadelphia. She, Anthony and Gage worked "16 hours day and night" to write and distribute copies of the Woman's Declaration of Rights. Again the story of Gage holding an umbrella to protect Anthony from the sun. Gage had to fight gender discrimination in her effort to rent an office for NWSA in Philadelphia.

Stanton credits Gage with assisting Anthony before her trial; mentions Gage's work on *History of Woman Suffrage* only in passing.

Stanton offers a backhanded apology to Gage who objected to Stanton's using her favorite phrase in autographs she signed without attribution. The phrase or motto read, "There is a word sweeter than mother, home or heaven. That word is Liberty." Noticeably annoyed and defensive, Stanton explains that the omission of Gage's name was inadvertent.

Stanton's book, *A Woman's Bible,* is described as just a compilation of references to women in the Bible with her commentaries. A reader would have no inkling on how much Stanton suffered from the attacks leveled by the members of NAWSA who were outraged by what they called her "heresy."

Stoddard Hope, *FAMOUS AMERICAN WOMEN* ©1970
The only suffragists included in this list of famous American women were Susan B. Anthony and Lucretia Mott. It is noteworthy that not only Gage, but also Stanton is omitted from this 1970 publication.

Wagner, Sally Roesch, *MATILDA JOSLYN GAGE: SHE WHO HOLDS THE SKY.* ©1998 and 2002
This is the first biography and history of Matilda Joslyn Gage written by a feminist historian using primary sources, documents, correspondence and regional publications. All the information about Gage is original to this monograph. Published by the Gage Foundation, it may have had limited distribution at the time of its publication. Wagner taught one of the nation's first women's studies class at California State University, Sacramento in 1969. Biographical information on Gage and the history of the suffrage movement are intertwined.

"She Who Holds the Sky" is the translation of the Haudensaunee (Iroquois) name given to Gage when she was adopted into the Wolf Clan of the Mohawk Nation in 1893.

Gage's frequent correspondence with son Thomas Clarkson indicates he was her confidante.

Many of the journal articles and speeches Gage wrote over several decades, were consolidated into publications that appeared in the 1870's. Among Gage's publications were:

Woman as Inventor which includes the story of the invention of the cotton gin, originally designed by Catherine Littlefield Greene. Greene declined to patent the cotton gin for fear of being ridiculed; thus Eli Whitney was given all the credit and fame.

Woman's Rights Catechism asserts that the federal government was responsible for the protection of human rights and had to overrule state laws that denied human rights.

Who Planned the Tennessee Campaign of 1862? Anna Ella Carroll vs. Ulysses S. Grant describes the story of Carroll's military strategy used for the Union's campaign in Tennessee during the Civil War. Active in Maryland Republican Party politics when her father was Governor, Carroll knew Lincoln as a friend. She originated the strategy used to defeat the Confederate Army. The author's identity was kept under wraps.

Woman, Church and State, Gage's "magnum opus," was published by a Socialist publishing company in Chicago. Wagner writes that Gage "never received proper acknowledgement of her co-authorship of the History of Woman Suffrage." 1876–1886 were the "busiest" years of Gage's life and included the writing of the History of Woman Suffrage. Gage's criticism of the church did not mean she was not religious. She challenged government contradictions. For example, if federal government could grant suffrage to convicted felons, why not women? Another contradiction: Anthony was tried in a federal court though elections were under states' jurisdiction. Gage was President of NWSA for only one year but served as chair of the Executive Committee for many years as well as editor and writer for the NWSA journal. She played a key role at the 1876 Centennial Celebration; was chosen to read an address to President Hayes during NWSA's 1879 Convention.

Gage's reputation was "principled to a fault..." "Conciliation was not a word in Gage's vocabulary." Her radicalism and persistence in the face of opposition caused Gage increasing isolation and rejection. Believes Anthony's power in NWSA pushed Gage into the recesses of the public face of the movement.

While Gage was in Dakota, Anthony took over her chairmanship of the Executive Committee in NWSA and arranged the merger with AWSA which included members of WCTU. Gage vehemently opposed WCTU and its charismatic president believing they would subvert both NWSA's equal rights position and eliminate its commitment to separation of church and state. WCTU lobbied for church/state alliance.

Wagner, Sally Roesch, *SISTERS IN SPIRIT: Haudenosaunee (Iroquois) Influence on Early American Feminists* ©2001
Haudenosaunee neighbors, with whom Gage and Stanton had friendships, inspired and confirmed the women's feminist vision of an egalitarian society. Gage had found matriarchal societies in the history of civilization, but a living example was right there in her own backyard.

Haudenosaunee women had civil, social and economic rights that included the right to choose and unseat the tribal chief, have primary custody of their children, share ownership of material goods, and end a marital relationship. The absence of male violence toward women and absence of rape contrasted sharply with Euro-American women who suffered from domestic violence. A society where women had equal rights was more than a utopian dream.

Wagner, Sally Roesch, *WONDERFUL MOTHER OF OZ*
©2003
Story of L.Frank Baum, Gage's son-in-law, their relationships
and mutual interests. Analysis of Oz as matriarchal utopia.
Matilda had originally opposed daughter Maud's decision to
marry Frank, but later became Baum's intellectual mentor.
Gage shared her intense interest in Theosophy and the books of
Madam Blavatsky with her family.

Ward, Geoffrey C. and Ken Burns, *NOT FOR OURSELVES
ALONE: the Story of Elizabeth Cady Stanton & Susan B. Anthony*
©1999
Contains content of TV documentary, Not for Ourselves Alone,
by Ken Burns. There are incidental references to Gage in eight
pages, but she was omitted from the Burns popular documentary.
Gage is described as "friend and ally,"…"suffragist writer
and organizer," an author of the 1876 Declaration, and the
person who held an umbrella over Anthony's head at the 1876
Centennial in Philadelphia. Writes that Stanton was late in
arriving in Philadelphia, which raises the unanswered question of
who was the primary author of the Declaration.
Gage was ill when Stanton wrote Volume II of the *History of
Woman Suffrage.* (Other source indicates Gage spent a month on
Vol. II.)

These authors believe that Stanton & Anthony are "responsible
for the largest social transformation in American history."
Points out that no information is available on the early
development of the Stanton/Anthony friendship in the months
that followed their first meeting in May, 1851.
This book has photo of the suffrage "triumvirate" at the
International Council of Women meeting in Washington D.C. -
shows Gage sitting next to Stanton.

Stanton and Gage wrote a public letter criticizing Anthony
for working too closely with women in WCTU who opposed
feminist interests. In 1890, WCTU had 150,000 members;
NAWSA had 13,000. Temperance women wore white ribbons
(for purity), later added yellow ribbons for suffrage.

Anthony refused request from Ida B. Wells-Barnett to form a chapter of NAWSA for Negro suffragists in 1894. And Wells was told not to walk with white women in the 1913 suffrage parade in Washington D. C. Concern for NAWSA's Southern white women constituency was a priority.
In 1900, only 4 states had suffrage: Wyoming, Utah, Colorado and Idaho.

Weatherford, Doris, *HISTORY OF THE AMERICAN SUFFRAGIST MOVEMENT* ©1998
A comprehensive history of the suffrage movement. Amplifies information found in other histories by describing social and political developments of the period in which the suffrage reform movement functioned. 1850's was age of experimentation; 1870's and '80's saw "explosion of organization building," to include study and civic clubs.

Women well represented at Columbian Exposition of 1892-93, compared to 1876. There they had the opportunity to network with other organizations such as the National Council of Jewish Women and American Nurses Association.

References to Gage are found in eleven pages but give significant recognition to Gage's importance to the movement. She had "moved far beyond her old friends in matters of feminist theory,"…"feared women were losing their cutting edge."
Gage was "movement's chief historian and most thoughtful intellectual"… "backbone" of the women's movement with Stanton and Anthony. Edited NWSA's journal, "National Citizen and Ballot Box," from 1878-81. Gage became "more ideologically radical as she aged." …wore "stylish clothes."

Gage went to Dakota to work for inclusion of women in new state constitutions when the territory was split. Gave her highest priority to keep the word "male" out of the 14th amendment. Volume IV of *History of Woman Suffrage* "devotes an excessive amount of attention to pageantry, pomp, and even floral decorations."

Woman Church and State was published at a time when conservatism flourished. Second generation of suffrage supporters was passive. Young women were not involved with the older leaders. Survey of Radcliffe students found only 2 of 72 women supported suffrage in 1898.

Gage died while writing a speech for the 50th anniversary of the Seneca Falls Convention. She was living with the Baums in Chicago the last two years of her life.

Wheeler, Marjorie Spruill, ed. *ONE WOMAN, ONE VOTE: Rediscovering the Woman Suffrage Movement* ©1995,1996
A collection of essays, three of which relate to the 19th century suffrage movement. Gage is not included in any of these essays. She is identified only as one of the editors of the *History of Woman Suffrage.*

The three essays are: "The Seneca Falls Convention" taken from the History of Woman Suffrage, "A Feminist Friendship" about Anthony and Stanton by Alice Rossi, and "Taking the Law Into Our Own Hands" on the Minor v. Happersett Supreme Court case by Ellen DuBois.
Wheeler admires Stanton: "There was probably not another woman in the nineteenth century who put her tongue and pen to better use than Stanton."

Frances E. Willard and Mary A. Livermore, ed. *A WOMAN OF THE CENTURY: 1470 Biographical Sketches Accompanied by Portraits of Leading American Women in All Walks of Life* ©1893
Gage biography in Vol. 3, pages 309-310.
This reference was written when the suffrage triumvirate was alive. Editors wrote that their work was unique because it filled a "vacant niche" in the reference library and that the "19th century was woman's century." "Since time began, no other era has witnessed so many and so great changes in the development of her character and gifts...."

Gage's resolutions in 1878 on woman and church were "too

radical for the great body of woman suffragists, creating a vast amount of discussion and opposition within NWSA." Authors list Gage's "most important" speeches: "Centralization," "United States Voters," "Woman in the Early Christian Church," and "Dangers of the Hour."

Brief summaries of biographies written for Gage, Anthony and Stanton that follow omit biographical data repeated in other sources. Summarized below are editorial comments for each of the three leaders.

GAGE
Confirms Gage's important leadership. Mother from "distinguished" Scottish family of conservative tradition. Paternal grandfather was a Patriot in American Revolution.
"From her earliest years, Matilda was accustomed to hearing the most abstruse political and religious questions discussed."
"From her pen have appeared many of the most able state papers (of NWSA) and addresses to the various political parties."
Gage wrote articles that were diatribes against the church prior to the publication of *Woman, Church and State.*

ANTHONY
Teacher at age 15; taught for 15 years. Organized NY State Temperance Association. Active abolitionist. Anthony believed that without the vote, women would be powerless.
Anthony is quoted as saying she has "no time to dip out vice with a teaspoon while the wrongly-adjusted forces of society are pouring it in by the bucketful."
(Anthony) "is one of the most heroic figures in American history. The future will place her name with the greatest of our statesmen." Refers to Anthony's arrest for voting, her trial and her regret that "she gave bonds which prevented her from going to the Supreme Court."

STANTON
"reformer and philanthropist ...orator, vigorous... She has the
mental force of a giant."
Wanted to make drunkenness legal cause for divorce. Stanton
attempted to cut out unjust laws from her father's law books
when she was a child. *New York Herald* supported her candidacy
for New York State's 8th Congressional District in 1868. She
received 24 votes.

AMERICAN NATIONAL BIOGRAPHY 1999 Volume 8 Entry
for Gage includes one page, for Anthony three pages, for Stanton
four pages. Gage attended Clinton Liberal Institute at age 15
after being home-schooled. President of both the NWSA and
NY State Suffrage Associations, 1875. Wrote and edited NWSA
newspaper. Described as "foremost leader" of woman suffrage
movement.

Contribution lies in her scholarship and historical writing.
Believed "misogynist elements of Christian doctrine major cause
of woman's lower social status." ..."recurrent invalidism."
Husband Henry Gage, dry goods merchant, said to have had
an estate valued at $60,000 in 1870. Matilda "thought to be
'dominant' partner in the marriage."

Sources: Leach; Willard and Livermore; *Obituaries in NY Times
and Chicago Tribune*, March 19,1898. Gage scrapbooks housed in
Library of Congress.
Entry written by Elizabeth Zoe Vacary.

DICTIONARY OF AMERICAN BIOGRAPHY 1931-2 and
1959-60, Volume 4
"Intellectually, (Gage) was without doubt among the ablest of the
suffrage leaders of the 19th century." She was one of the "strong-
minded" women of her age ..."one of the foremost leaders of the
women's suffrage movement." Her writings and intellect were her
most important contribution.

Authored 1876 Women's Declaration of Rights with

Stanton and Anthony, read at the Centennial Celebration on Independence Day. Published *Woman, Church and State* 1893. Gage instrumental in achieving women's vote in school board elections in New York State.

Sources: *History of Woman Suffrage; Life and Work of Susan B. Anthony* by Harper; "Onondaga's Centennial" 1896; Boston and Chicago journals; Leach; Willard and Livermore. Obituaries in NY Times and Chicago Tribune, March 19,1898.
Entry written by W. Randall Waterman.

NOTABLE AMERICAN WOMEN VOLUME II ©1973 Duplicates much of the content in *DICTIONARY OF AMERICAN BIOGRAPHY*. Gage retained membership in Fayetteville Baptist Church. Great interest in Theosophy. Disagreed with husband Henry in 1872 election. Matilda supported Grant against Greeley who had conservative views on suffrage.

Rediscovery of Gage's work by scholars is gradually re-establishing her reputation as one of the most influential voices among nineteenth century woman reformers. "Lacked sparkling personality of Stanton."

Two years of invalidism from heart disease before her death. Died of embolism in brain. Remains buried in Fayetteville. Favorite motto on gravestone: "There is a word sweeter than mother, home or heaven. That word is Liberty."

Anthony wrote to son Thomas Clarkson Gage praising his mother as "one of most intensely earnest, true women we have ever had in our movement. Had she been possessed of a strong constitution…she would have done more for the emancipation of women than all the rest of us put together. With her feeble health, she accomplished wonders."

Sources: Gage papers in Schlessinger Library and other libraries; Willard and Livermore; Biography of Lillie Devereux Blake; obituaries. Entry written by Elizabeth Warbasse.

INTERNET REFERENCES

MATILDA JOSLYN GAGE FOUNDATION Fayetteville, NY. Website permits a virtual tour of the Gage home. www.matildajoslyngage.org
Among the Gage Foundation's publications for purchase is "The Reader Series." It includes Fayetteville's First Woman Voter (Rivette) "Dangers of the Hour" (Gage's speech to the Woman's National Liberal Union) Wonderful Mother of Oz (Wagner) and Woman as Inventor (Gage).

"A WOMAN OF THE CENTURY: 1,470 Biographical Sketches Accompanied by Portraits of Leading American Women in All Walks of Life," Willard and Livermore, editors 1893
http://books.google.com/books?id=zXEEAAAAYAAJ&pg=PA 309&dq=%22A+Woman+of+the+Century%22+Matilda+Joslyn+ Gage&hl=en&ei=M4VVTfDwJ8TYgAfCgaGpDQ&sa=X&oi= book_result&ct=result&resnum=1&ved=0CCsQ6AEwAA#v=on epage&q&f=false

STANTON/ANTHONY PAPERS PROJECT, Gordon, Ann D., editor, Rutgers University, 1997
This project to organize and later digitize the Stanton/Anthony papers began in 1982. See Bibliography entry under Gordon. http://ecssba.rutgers.edu/

HISTORY OF WOMAN SUFFRAGE, Anthony, Stanton, Gage, editors; Kindle edition, 2012.

"EARLY SUFFRAGE PROTESTS: Miss Blake Tells of Meeting at Statue of Liberty 29 Years Ago." New York Times, July 11, 1915.
http://query.nytimes.com/mem/archive-free/pdf?res=F50813FA 3C5D17738DDDA80994DF405B858DF1D3

Bernikow, Louise *"The Statue of Liberty and Early Feminism"* June 25, 2003.

http://www.womensenews.org/story/our-story/030625/the-statue-liberty-and-early-feminism

"Matilda Joslyn Gage, Women's Rights Activist," Woman of Courage Profile written and produced by the St. Lawrence County, New York branch of the American Association of University Women. Apparently posted 1998.
http://www.northnet.org/stlawrenceaauw/gage.htm

Fenton, Zanita, *"No Witch is a Bad Witch: A Commentary on the Erasure of Matilda Joslyn Gage."*

"Part of the Law and Literature symposium, Taking Oz Seriously, held at Albany Law School in November 2009. The Fenton Essay focuses on the life of Matilda Joslyn Gage, mother-in-law of The Wonderful Wizard of Oz author, L. Frank Baum. It also uses the text of *The Wonderful Wizard of Oz*, to explore the nature of power (or the illusion of it) and hierarchy, especially in organizations which seek progressive objectives."
http://papers.ssrn.com/sol3/papers.cfm?abstract_id=1713930
Southern California Interdisciplinary Law Journal, Vol. 20, 2010
University of Miami Legal Studies Research Paper No. 2010-35

MATILDA JOSLYN GAGE
TIMELINE

1826 Born in Cicero, New York

1845 Marries Henry Gage, eight years her senior, in January

1845 Daughter Helen Leslie Gage born in November

1848 Thomas Clarkson Gage born in July

1849 Charles Henry Gage born in December,
        died one month later

1851 Julia Louise Gage born in April

1852 Attends Syracuse Convention with seven year old
        daughter Helen. Gage's speech there is the only existing
        text of all her speeches.

1854 Family moves from Manlius to Fayetteville

1860 Suspension of suffrage activism during Civil War

1861 Daughter Maud born in March

1869 Co-founder National Woman Suffrage Association.
        Editor of NWSA journal, *"National Citizen &
        Ballot Box"* for three years. Holds Executive positions in
        NWSA leadership with Anthony and Stanton.
        Initiates NY State Woman's Suffrage Association.
        President for 9 years, executive positions for 20 years.

1872 Anthony's trial for voting illegally
        Victoria Woodhull runs for President

1874 Supreme Court decision: Minor v. Happersett

1876 "Woman's Declaration of Rights" for Centennial
        Celebration

1876-86 Co-editor with Stanton and Anthony, *History of
        Woman Suffrage*, Volumes I – III

1878 First introduction of suffrage amendment in Congress

1880 Women win right to vote in NY State school board
        elections

1881 Helen's home wedding (April) Marries 8th cousin

Charles H. Gage

1882 Julia's home wedding (Feb.) Marries James D. Carpenter
Maud's home wedding (Nov.) Marries L. Frank Baum

1884 Henry Gage dies

1885 Son Thomas Clarkson marries Sophie Taylor Jewell in
Aberdeen, Dakota

1886 Joins protest at Statue of Liberty Dedication, Bedloe's
Island, NY City

1888 Helps organize International Council of Women meeting
in Washington, D.C.

1890 Merger of AWSA and NWSA
Gage organizes Women's National Liberal Union
NY State school board suffrage overturned

1893 Completes *"Woman Church and State"* – her "magnum
opus."

1893 Adopted into Mohawk nation (member of
Iroquois Confederation)

1896 Becomes critically ill. Spends last two years of her life
with the Baums

1898 Gage dies in Chicago at Maud and Frank Baum's home

1913 Alice Paul leads Woman's Suffrage Parade, Washington
D.C.

1920 Passage of 19th Amendment to the
Constitution for woman suffrage.

LAST WILL

MATILDA JOSLYN GAGE 1826-1898
Submitted by Kathy Crowell

ONONDAGA COUNTY

Last Will of Matilda J. Gage (Liber 10, Page 72):

Know all men by these presents, that I, Matilda Joslyn Gage of
Fayetteville, Onondaga County, State of New York, considering
the uncertainty of life and being of sound and disposing
mind and memory do make and publish this my last Will and
Testament, hereby revoking and making null and void all other
last wills and testaments by me heretofore made. First. I desire
that my body shall be cremated as I deem cremation to be a
much more deemly and healthful method of disposing of the
body than that of burial in the ground. Second. After my funeral
expenses and all my just and lawful debts have been paid and
discharged I give and bequeath all of my property, consisting of
real estate both in the State of New York and in the Territory
of Dakota stocks, bonds, notes and accounts and other personal
property, to be equally divided share and share alike between my
four children Mrs. Helen Leslie Gage, P. (sic) Clarkson Gage,
Julia Louise Gage Carpenter and Maud Gage Baum. And I wish
it to be understood as my will that in case of the death of either
one of my children without natural heirs, the portion that would
have belonged to such child shall be equally divided between
my other surviving children, or in case but one survives, and no
natural heir or heirs have been left by either of the others then
that one surviving child shall take the whole. It is my express
will that my house in Fayetteville, now occupied by me as a
residence shall be kept and used as a home without the payment
of rent as long as Helen Leslie Gage, or any other one of my
children desires to use it for a home and residence; the child or

children occupying it shall keep the house and barn fully insured for the benefit of the estate in the amount they are ordinarily insured for, and this is to be done at the sole expense of the child or children occupying it as a home. Such child or children so occupying it shall also pay all taxes levied upon the place, and keep up all necessary repairs upon the house and barn, and shall also keep up the flower garden at their own sole expense as long as occupying it as a home, and the above payment of insurance, taxes and repairs shall be considered by the other heirs as in lieu of rent. At the end of six years from and after my death the home shall either be sold and the proceeds equally divided between my surviving children, or if longer desired as a residence, the child or children so desiring to use it, shall pay to the other heirs the portion due them upon its assessed valuation by my executors who, upon this payment being made, shall then legally release the premises to the child, or children continuing to occupy it as a residence. I desire that my books and silver shall be divided among my children as they can agree, but to my youngest daughter, Maud Gage Baum, if living at time of my decease, I give and bequeath all of my woman suffrage papers, books and documents of whatever character except my scrap books, which latter I desire that she shall deposit in some permanent public library. I hereby give full power of attorney to my representatives authorizing them to convey real estate, and empower them to lease the same from month to month and year to year. I do this especially to avoid the expense of probating my will. I hereby make, constitute and appoint my beloved children Helen Leslie Gage, T. Clarkson Gage, Julia Louise Gage Carpenter and Maude Gage Baum as executors of my estate neither of whom shall be required to give bonds. And if all do not qualify, I desire that those who do shall make no charge to the other legatees for their service farther than the actual expense they may be put to in the settlement of my estate but consider themselves paid by the portion, coming to them and should there be any legal dispute among or between my children in reference to the provisions of my will be deemed disinherited, and the portion, or portions that otherwise would have been hers his or theirs shall be equally divided between the others. In Witness whereof,

I have hereunto subscribed my name and set my hand and seal this seventh day of September, one thousand and eight hundred and eighty five. Matilda Joslyn Gage insignia. Signed, sealed published and declared by the said Matilda Joslyn Gage, in our presence to be her last will and testament, who at her request and in her presence and in the presence of each other have hereunto subscribed our names as witnesses. Chas. Baker, Fayetteville Onondaga Co., N.Y., Adelia Baker, Fayetteville Onondaga Co., N.Y. State of New York county of Onondaga Surrogate's Office so I, Michael M. Mara, Clerk, of the Surrogate's Court of the County of Onondaga New York do hereby certify that the annexed instrument is a copy of the last will and testament of Matilda Joslyn Gage, late of the Village of Fayetteville in said County of Onondaga, deceased, which said last will and testament was by a decree of the Surrogate's Court of the said county of Onondaga, bearing date the 11th day of July, 1898 admitted to probate and record in said Court, as a will valid to pass both real and personal estate. That I have compared said copy with the original record of said estate now in my custody and that the same is a true transcript therefrom and of the whole thereof (insignia). $.10 U.S.I.R. Canceled. In Testimony whereof, I have hereunto set my hand and affixed the seal of the Surrogate's Court of the County of Onondaga, at the Surrogate's Office, in the City of Syracuse in said county, this 1st day of April 1901. M. M. Mara, Clerk of the Surrogate Court. Recorded April 1, 1901 at 10:50 a. m. Jos. E. Hubbell, Clerk.

On the stone monument erected at her cremation site in Fayetteville Cemetery is the inscription:

MATILDA JOSLYN GAGE   1826 - 1898

There is a word sweeter than mother
home or heaven — that word is Liberty

http://www.rootsweb.ancestry.com/~nyononda/COURT/W10P72.HTM

OBITUARY

Obituary in The Weekly Recorder (Fayetteville, NY) March 24, 1898:

Mrs. Matilda J. Gage died in Chicago, on Friday, aged 72 years. Mrs. Gage was one of the earliest champions of woman's rights in America, having identified herself with that movement in 1852. For many years she was president of the New York State Woman's Suffrage Association. In 1878 she formed the Woman's National Liberal League, being elected president, which positions she had since held. Mrs. Gage was associated with Mrs. Stanton and Miss Anthony in the authorship of *"The History of Woman's Suffrage,"* and was the editor of the National Citizen, published at Syracuse from 1878 to 1882. The most important work of her life, however, as she herself considered, was consummated in the publication three years ago of her book, *"Woman, Church and State."*

Mrs. Gage was the daughter of Dr. Hezekiah Joslyn of Cicero, in this county, where she was born March 24th 1826.

Her father was a man of profound thought and a thorough student of all new questions. His home was a station on the underground railroad, and the home of anti-slavery speakers and advanced thinkers on every subject, as well as the clergymen who often came to hold meetings in the place.

Matilda was always allowed to listen to the conversation of her father's guests, and it was a law with him that all her childish questions should be reasonably answered.

Listening to the discussions of her father and the clergymen upon religious subjects she was early converted and united with the church at eleven years of age.

In after years she had less regard for any formal religion, though she retained a nominal membership in the church the greater portion of her life, her name having been retained on the roll of membership of the Fayetteville Baptist church the past thirty-five years. She never lost faith in the old fundamental truths of religion, and while not adopting in full the theories of any of the new schools of thought, she claimed to be an investigator on those fields, especially of psychology and theosophy.

Her father was her instructor in mathematics, Greek and physiology, and at the same time taught her what she most prized, to think for herself. She received her later instruction in DeRuyter and Hamilton.

From her mother, a Scotch lady of the old and influential family of Leslie, she inherited a taste for delving into old histories and writings.

She was married in 1845 to Henry H. Gage, a merchant, with whom she soon removed to Manlius, where she was the sole representation of the woman's suffrage movement.

After a short residence in Manlius, Mr. and Mrs. Gage located in Fayetteville. She had a family of children, yet her pen was ever at work upon the suffrage movement. She had served as president and vice-president of both the state and national organizations of woman's suffrage.

During the rebellion she was one of the most enthusiastic workers in Fayetteville in preparing hospital supplies for the soldiers and in 1862 predicted the failure of any course of defense and maintenance of the Union that did not free the slaves.

When Company C, 122d Regt., N.Y., S. Vols., was leaving for the war, Mrs. Gage presented to them, in an appropriate and patriotic address, a national flag; during which address she wrapped the flag about her, referring impressively to its symbolism of protection and freedom, and passed it to them amid the enthusiasm of the company and of the people who had gathered to bid them a good bye.
In 1876 at the approach of the presidential campaign Mrs. Gage, Lillie Devereux Blake and Dr. Clemence S. Lozier prepared

an appeal to the legislature asking for suffrage for women in the presidential election, an action within its power without a constitutional amendment. After presentation to the legislature the appeal was referred to the judiciary committee and though reported unfavorably and never reaching a vote, the little consideration given it was again over former years, when a plea of such a nature was hardly noticed.

In 1880, when school suffrage was given in this state to women, Mrs. Gage led a company of women in her own village and was the first woman to cast a ballot, helping to elect the first woman school trustee in this state.

Mrs. Gage was a lecturer and writer well known throughout the country. Her books aside from those mentioned above are, "Woman as Inventor," "Who Planned the Tennessee Campaign?" Woman's Rights Catechism." She had a distinctive personality, decided convictions, independence of thought and action, a courage of opinion, was gifted in the use of language, a forceful speaker and with all had a warm and sympathizing nature which made her a friend and help to the poor and a kind neighbor.

The strength of her convictions and her fearlessness in enunciating them, radical as many of them were, of course provoked antagonisms, and yet none but would recognize her honesty and sincerity, and she commanded the respect of those who did not adopt her views. Her...commanded attention and respect in any sphere in which she moved. Since the death of her husband, Sept. 16, 1884, and the marriage of her children one after another, Mrs. Gage has spent only a portion of time here, but has kept up the old home, and was happy in the anticipation of returning to it soon, when the summons came and she passed on to the home beyond. She is survived by four children, Mrs. Helen Leslie Gage, widow of the late Charles H. Gage, of Aberdeen, N.D., Mrs. James Carpenter of Fargo, S.D., Clarkson T. Gage, of Bloomington, Ill. and Mrs. Frank Baum, of Chicago, where Mrs. Gage died.

http://www.rootsweb.ancestry.com/~nyononda/OBITUARY/GAGEMJ.HTM

ABOUT THE AUTHOR

Charlotte Shapiro taught American Studies and Government in Rockville Centre, New York, for 13 years, while raising three children. Her second career was in community advocacy for women's equality in the workplace. She co-founded the equal employment rights agency, Women on the Job with Lillian McCormick in Port Washington, New York in 1981.

Shapiro and her profile of Women on the Job are in Long Island Women Activists and Innovators, Hofstra University, Long Island Institute Publication, edited by Natalie A. Naylor and Maureen O. Murphy. 1998. Women on the Job's papers (1981 – 2005) are archived in the Robert E. Wagner Labor Library of New York University.

Research, writing and editing have been a staple of Shapiro's career since her work on the first edition of the *Comparative Guide to American Colleges,* by James Cass and Max Birnbaum, 1964 and *Parents' Guide to Summer Camps*, by Charlotte M. Shapiro and Lore Jarmul, 1968.

Shapiro joined the League of Women Voters (heir to the National American Woman Suffrage Association) serving as League president in Levittown and Nassau County; Board Member in the New York State League of Women Voters.

19541792R00063

Made in the USA
Charleston, SC
30 May 2013